CAREERS FOR

THE STAGE-
STRUCK
& Other Dramatic Types

VGM Careers for You Series

CAREERS FOR

THE STAGE-STRUCK

& Other Dramatic Types

LUCIA MAURO

SECOND EDITION

VGM Career Books

Chicago   New York   San Francisco   Lisbon   London   Madrid   Mexico City
Milan   New Delhi   San Juan   Seoul   Singapore   Sydney   Toronto

The *McGraw·Hill* Companies

Library of Congress Cataloging-in-Publication Data

Mauro, Lucia
    Careers for the stagestruck & other dramatic types / Lucia Mauro— 2nd ed.
      p.   cm. — (VGM careers for you series)
    ISBN 0-07-141157-7 (alk. paper)
      1. Performing arts—Vocational guidance.   I. Title: Careers for the
stagestruck and other dramatic types.   II. Title.   III. Series.

    PN1580.M38   2004
    791'.023—dc22   2003025816

1 2 3 4 5 6 7 8 9 0   LBM/LBM   3 2 1 0 9 8 7 6 5 4

ISBN 0-07-141157-7

McGraw-Hill books are available at special quantity discounts to use as premiums
and sales promotions, or for use in corporate training programs. For more
information, please write to the Director of Special Sales, Professional Publishing,
McGraw-Hill, Two Penn Plaza, New York, NY 10121-2298. Or contact your local
bookstore.

This book is printed on acid-free paper.

To Joe, my leading man . . .
and guiding light

Contents

Foreword

··

Wh
hen Lucia Mauro recently asked me to revise the
Foreword for the second edition of her book *Careers for
the Stagestruck & Other Dramatic Types*, I was amazed
when I realized how much time had passed since that initial edition! A great deal has changed in the world since 1997, and the
same holds true in the world of the performing arts. For example,
the technological advances made in theatrical design alone would
be enough to make your head spin. Yet Ms. Mauro's overall argument remains true: If you plan to pursue a career in the performing arts, you must get the proper training and continue to study
throughout your lifetime.

In this practical guide for the stagestruck and other dramatic
types, Ms. Mauro covers theatre, music, opera, dance, theatrical
design, teaching, and writing. Her insights are informative and
valuable to anyone getting ready to launch his or her career. As the
former owner/instructor of the Actors' Center, a professional
acting studio in Chicago, I found that some beginning students
wanted to become actors overnight. Attempting to go on stage
without the proper education, these students failed to realize that
it not only takes extensive instruction but also hard work and
dedication to the craft. This book stresses that, no matter what
artistic occupation you finally choose, it is necessary to get that
training . . . and continue to study, work, and practice. This kind
of ongoing effort is essential for anyone who strives to be an actor,

singer, dancer, musician, designer, teacher, or writer. The vast challenges of these demanding professions simply require it.

When I first read the book, I found myself a bit jealous. I wish I had had this practical book as a resource when I was a student, so I could have explored the breadth and depth of various performance-based professions. In college, I chose the path of the theatre director. More recently, I went back to school to obtain a master's degree in Irish theatre from Trinity College Dublin. I also will pursue doctoral studies in theatre at the University of Minnesota, Minneapolis. While higher education may not be the path chosen, continual training and learning in one way or another is critically important to those on stage and behind the scenes.

Without hesitation, I only have the highest recommendation for this book as a resource manual. It gives the reader an opportunity to learn about many different career paths in theatre, opera, dance, or music. If you have interests in any of these areas, take a closer look inside these pages to find out where your true calling lies. If you are willing to work hard and make the necessary commitment, a life in the performing arts can be an exciting and rewarding profession.

This book will help send you on your way!

Kay Martinovich
Associate Director
Irish Repertory of Chicago

CHAPTER ONE

Let's Put on a Show!

Long before Judy Garland and Mickey Rooney belted out the now-legendary theatrical battle cry, "Let's put on a show!" the decidedly stagestruck and dramatic types of yore were struttin' their stuff. Evidence from cave paintings indicates that dances and pantomime were closely connected to religious or agricultural rituals. The ancient Greeks and Romans were performing their Aeschylus and Horace against a colonnaded backdrop. The gods, of course, all played an instrument. And ballet dancers bowed before Catherine de Médici during the Italian Renaissance, while Shakespeare's traveling band of players entertained an awestruck Queen Elizabeth I.

Over the centuries, the performing arts have evolved into a structured, all-inclusive industry that employs over one million professionals across the country. Despite decreased funding from the National Endowment for the Arts, the profession has experienced a steady rise in career opportunities. Theatre and dance companies have been challenged to get creative with their marketing and fund-raising strategies. And a dedicated core of educators is ensuring that outstanding training continues to be available. Arts programs at all levels of education are tailored toward an individual's special interests and skills. They are balanced with field trips, internships, and performing experience.

Although most aspiring entertainers have their hearts set on the silver screen, experts agree that stage experience is a necessary foundation to hone skills. It is also an incredibly rewarding career in itself. This book focuses on live performing opportunities, whose acquired skills can easily be carried over to the film industry. The most obvious difference between the stage and screen is that the former involves an on-the-spot audience that gives immediate feedback, while the latter includes several retakes—often shot out of sequence—in an environment that separates the audience from the actors.

Regardless, a career in the performing arts involves erratic hours, constant practice, fluctuating pay, and varying degrees of egos. Talent is key, but you also must exhibit drive, determination, confidence, and, most importantly, respect toward your peers. Competition can inspire or deflate an individual's spirit. Some of the most successful performers are those who take charge of their careers while working collaboratively with fellow artists.

Divas still exist. Yet they are more the exception than the rule these days. The performing arts field is so expansive that you can certainly discover where you would feel most comfortable and fulfilled. And here's the beautiful part: if you don't quite fit into the categories listed, create your own! That's how flexible and open-ended this profession is.

Remember, too, that the arts are a business. You may be the most creative person in the world, but if you don't know how to market your work or make a profit, your resources will simply dry up. Or worse, no one will come out to see you perform. Team up with savvy arts professionals and join arts organizations that will assist you with the overall management of a career with no set pay scale or corporate ladder climbing.

Finding new audiences and keeping loyal subscribers are ongoing issues across the board in this field, and seminars on these subjects have grown in popularity. Many artists are forced to go above and beyond the call when promoting themselves. Interestingly, as arts awareness grows, more companies and venues sprout up—leaving audiences with more options but still not enough time to fit all the choices into their busy schedules. The average viewer will prioritize and budget, making the competition even more fierce.

Philip J. Santora, managing director of Chicago's Northlight Theatre, believes arts organizations must devise more creative ways to approach potential funders. "If you look at the current arts climate," he says, "contributed income tends to go toward a specific product rather than general operating expenses. So you can commission new works, but it's difficult to pay the theatre's light bill."

Before joining Northlight in 2003, Santora served as managing director of the Georgia Shakespeare Festival for seven years. When Santora arrived at the not-for-profit Georgia Shakespeare Festival in 1995, it was a $500,000 operation with three Shakespearean plays running in rotating repertory under a circus tent. By 1997, he was instrumental in the construction of the theatre's $6 million facility, the Conant Performing Arts Center. He ran two successful capital campaigns and set up a cash reserve. Today Georgia Shakespeare Festival is the second-largest theatre in the state, with a $1.25 million budget and an expanded performing season.

Now at Northlight Theatre, Santora is in the midst of mapping out a growth plan that will involve staff, board, and the community. He also aims to expand the theatre's education programs: "We're being truly community responsive. We need to talk to teachers and to parents."

On the financial side, goals include building an endowment and creating innovative funding strategies in these challenging economic times. And he's ready to face some of the greater challenges of the twenty-first century.

"At Georgia Shakespeare," Santora contends, "our competition was not other Shakespearean theatres. It was new restaurants, kids' activities, the Internet, movies, and just a night at home with the family. Now it's harder to come out and see live theatre, but it's more and more important because of how insular our lives are."

In this book, you will learn about careers in theatre, dance, music, behind-the-scenes design and management, education, and publicity. You will also be given a chance to explore how these career choices often intersect. Overall, it's the well-rounded artist who can not only put on a show, but also allow the audience to carry away a substantial part of the magic and life lessons promoted by those glorious stage productions.

From the Top

We've all been fed Hollywood copy about how Betty Grable was discovered in a New York department store or how Tony Danza, a prizefighter at the Golden Gloves competition, got spotted by the producer of *Taxi*. But the scores of actors, dancers, and musicians getting regular work rarely have such colorful "discovery" stories to tell. Many begin training at a young age—often catching the acting bug during the grade school holiday pageant or from attending a live performance. Others cite their "fabulous high school drama teachers," who pointed them to the best college performing arts programs.

There's no getting around it: live performing involves a lot of hard work. Sure, it's a demanding life. For young performers, it means giving up a part of their childhoods to pursue a monumental dream—whether performing all the Bach violin concertos at Carnegie Hall or starring as Bialystock or Bloom in *The Producers*. It's important for aspiring performers to practice their chosen profession with intensity while having totally unrelated outlets. World-class violinist Rachel Barton, for example, listens to heavy metal music when she's not perfecting Mozart.

Movie star Tony Curtis—who has been touring the country in the stage musical version of *Some Like It Hot*—gets in touch with his emotions through painting bright Matisse-like canvases. "I mix colors the way I feel—not by some rules," Curtis told me in an interview. "Painting for me is an unspoken language. It's an extension of feelings; acting is an extension of ideas."

Research is vital when choosing an arts program, workshop, or school. In any of the performing arts categories, an insufficient training program can destroy a career, mainly because so much must be relearned. It's easier to start with a clean slate than to have to break out of bad habits. Get a lot of solid background information on instructors, who should willingly refer you to former students or invite you to observe a class. Don't devote all your energy to one style of instruction, either. Seek out diverse experiences.

Triple-threat talent (singers, dancers, actors) are still very much in demand. They have even extended beyond these traditional skills. Cirque du Soleil—the theatre-circus phenomenon that originated in Montreal—requires its artists to do daredevil acrobatics, clown, act, sing, dance, play an instrument and, sometimes, perform underwater. Other famed fusion spectacles include Blue Man Group, *Riverdance*, and *Stomp*.

Participate in master classes, attend free cultural events, and perform as much as possible. Your local park district is an excellent place to begin training, before moving on to reputable schools. Getting photographs (they're called "head shots" or "composites" in the biz) and signing up with a well-researched talent agency are smart strategies for nudging your foot—and whole body, for that matter—past the stage door.

There are many opportunities for child performers with exceptional talent, amiable personalities, and mature attitudes. Professionals in charge of the children's division of talent agencies screen prospective companies holding auditions. Parents should be involved in a practical, understanding, noncontrolling way. Stage moms went out about the same time vaudeville folded.

Today, a lot of dads are involved in their children's performing careers, too. Depending on the parents' schedules and occupations, many work out arrangements in which they can be paged or reached on their cell phones when their child gets an audition request. Friends and other family members are instrumental as part of the entire support system. Not all child entertainers go on to become adult stars, but the experience alone can help them become more outgoing, open-minded, disciplined, and responsible.

Other important starting points include attending live performances, listening to music, and observing master classes. Participating in arts-related conventions and special summer programs is also tremendously beneficial. The more art you are exposed to, the more comfortable you feel actually pursuing a career in the field. You will inevitably network and must keep your name out there. And know that producers, directors, conductors, and dance professionals always seek out fine talent. It's up to you to be seen and heard.

Are You Ready for Your Close-Up?

In tribute to Norma Desmond, the faded movie queen from the screen and stage versions of *Sunset Boulevard,* as she descends her massive Gothic staircase, we ask you, "Are you ready for your close-up?" As a performer, be aware that you do not hold a job. You are your job. You will live, breathe, eat, and sleep your chosen profession. So prepare yourself for an intense but extremely satisfying lifestyle.

Before the scent of greasepaint overwhelms you, make sure you are well suited to a performing artist's frenetic but invigorating lifestyle. An agreeable personality and balanced disposition are as important as your legato or grand jetés—if not more so.

As you prepare to pose for your quintessential publicity shot, ask yourself the following ten questions. They will indeed help you determine if a close-up is in order.

1. Are you focused, driven, and confident?
2. Do you compare yourself to others and let others indirectly determine your strengths and weaknesses for you?
3. Are you competitive in a healthy, nonthreatening way?
4. Does the idea of sharing your knowledge and experience with others appeal to you?
5. Who would you cite as role models and why?

6. What kinds of short- and long-term goals have you set for yourself?
7. Are you willing to work hard and devote long hours to perfecting your skills?
8. How do you react to criticism or handle rejection?
9. Do you consider yourself a flexible person?
10. Does the prospect of travel excite you?

Now review your reactions in light of the profession's realities. Being focused will open so many doors for you. Sure, it's great to be an all-around performer. However, there will come a point when zeroing in on what you do best could get you a substantial amount of work in a specific area. Being a concert pianist, a classical ballet dancer, and a dramatic actress is impressive, yet at some point these roles will conflict. That statement is not meant to discourage you from getting a well-rounded education. It's just a gentle warning to get you to concentrate on what specific aspect of the performing arts appeals to you most and for which area you feel well suited.

Drive and confidence allow you to believe that anything is possible. Successful performers rarely, if ever, do things halfway. Some of the best performers are capable of combining assertiveness with a relaxed sense of inner strength. Egos go only so far in this increasingly collaborative business.

While it may be incredibly tempting to compare yourself to other aspiring artists—especially during auditions—don't make a habit of it. You are who you are. Others have their strengths; you have yours. Constant comparisons often lead to discouragement. Of course, it's wise to look at the competition and even make note of areas in your own performance that need improvement. But letting others indirectly reveal what they think are your shortcomings can only be harmful. Get expert opinions before determining that you can never be as good as so and so. You will most likely change your way of thinking rather quickly.

This idea feeds right into the competitive nature of the arts and entertainment arena. In order to keep on your toes and in sync with industry changes, you've got to have an inherently competitive spirit. But when competition gets ruthless, it can virtually destroy an artist, who may become more obsessed with being "number one" than being the best at what he or she does. Performing is not about winning; it's about inspiring! Compete in a healthy, nonthreatening way with the only player who really matters—yourself.

We talked about the stage as fostering collaborative relationships. Sharing your knowledge and experience with your peers and other prospective artists is an enlightened strategy for helping the arts continue to flourish. About 90 percent of all performers are also teachers, in some measure. In the music field, artists often hold master classes during their tour stops. Dancers must learn proper technique from other dancers. And many actors are also directors and instructors.

These teachers often become role models for their students, who carry tips, phrases, adages, or ideas from their school days with them forever. Finding disciplined role models with strong values and a willingness to maintain professionalism in the arts is a step in the right direction. Aspiring to be like someone you admire—while not relinquishing your own identity—can only push you forward.

As you progress in your field of interest, set short-term goals that will get you to the next level. These little objectives will undoubtedly help you arrive at your long-ranging dreams. Violinist Rachel Barton offers this insight: "It's actually more fun when students are not held back by limitations. They don't get stuck in a rut at a certain level. No matter what someone's long-term goals are, if they don't advance, it's like treading water."

Hard work and long hours naturally go with the territory. Constant practice is essential to reaching perfection. Continue to challenge your body and mind for maximum performance.

The critics are not the only ones in a position to cheer or shriek at your performance. Teachers, peers, and audience members are also observing and judging your abilities. Steel yourself for the constructive criticism and make it a point to improve. On the other hand, do not stand for harmful personal attacks. Know the difference between the critics who want to help you improve and the ones who are just wielding some hefty power. Considering that you will be attending countless auditions, don't expect to be called back after every one. Many times, the rejection has nothing to do with your ability. The director may be seeking a certain type or "look" for a particular role.

By being a mentally flexible person, you can easily adapt to a variety of situations. In an unpredictable, constantly changing creative profession, flexibility goes hand-in-hand with opportunity. Now, if you're a dancer, being physically flexible is also a plus!

Rarely do performers stay in one place. If you're part of a touring company, you will obviously do a lot of traveling. In fact, it's highly likely that you will make regular appearances around the world no matter which area of the performing arts you choose.

Feel free to ask yourself more pressing, introspective questions about lifestyle and self-esteem. If you've given your career choice substantial thought, you will be leaps and bounds ahead of those who choose to "wing it" or flit about the field in dilettante-like vagueness.

A Sampling of Performing Arts Careers

So many areas of the performing arts intersect. As a musical theatre director, for instance, you will head a team of actors, dancers, musicians, and designers. Your shared vision ultimately brings a production to life. Educators in this field also have extensive hands-on performing experience. And even most arts writers and publicity professionals have been directly involved in an art form, such as music or dance.

Following are brief descriptions of the specific careers we explore in this book.

Careers in Theatre

The theatrical world encompasses a wealth of talented individuals who, together, essentially bring words and music to life. Actors come instantly to mind. After all, they are the ones in the limelight. And there are many different types of actors. Some train specifically for dramas or comedies, musical theatre, mime, or improvisation. Some are performance artists—solo performers who create experimental original material that combines different art forms in order to address deep sociopolitical and psychological issues. Actors, in general, entertain and educate audiences around the world.

Heading for the Great White Way is not as popular as it once was due to increased production costs in New York. A significant change has been the regional theatre movement, which continues to spread performing opportunities across the nation. The Big Apple is still considered the performing arts capital of America, but Chicago, Washington, D.C., San Francisco, and Minneapolis–St. Paul are other serious theatre cities, as are Toronto, Montreal, and Vancouver in Canada. Los Angeles has theatre, but it often serves as a showcase for actors more interested in getting discovered by a film talent scout than gaining recognition on the stage. Los Angeles attracts the celluloid set—and rightfully so. All the necessary filmmaking resources are there.

Directors essentially interpret scripts. They give their shows a voice. As their title implies, they direct the day-to-day details of script reading, rehearsal, design, and countless other activities. Sometimes directors also serve as producers—meaning they also finance their own work. But it's more common for a producer to be a separate financing entity, responsible for hiring and negotiating contracts. Stage managers also assist directors with production duties.

Playwrights create the scripts, which are typically "work-shopped" (or given staged readings) before they are revised and crafted into a substantial theatrical work. They collaborate closely with directors and producers. Unlike novelists, essayists, or journalists, playwrights must master a specific dialogue-driven writing style, which takes into consideration set and costume changes as well as the blocking of actors on stage and the pacing of a live performance.

A dramaturg is either a freelance or resident historian for a theatrical troupe. This highly specialized profession involves expertise in language and linguistics, rhythm, movement, historic events, particular eras, and dress. For period accuracy, dramaturgs are indispensable.

A frequently overlooked career is that of puppeteer—a complex specialization involving acute mechanical and building skills as well as the dexterity to be the voices for multisized puppets while manipulating their movements. Europe and Asia have long puppet traditions. But over the last fifteen years, theatre departments in North America have increased their puppetry courses. A common misconception is that puppet shows are only for children. But now it is not unusual to find outstanding puppet versions of famous adult-oriented plays or new works being written for the puppet booth.

Take, for example, the international tour of *Shockheaded Peter,* which originated in England. It is a wildly successful adult puppet spectacle inspired by a nineteenth-century book chronicling outrageous punishments for unruly children. Another example is Chicago, which has its own avant-garde Puppetry Festival sponsored by the city's Department of Cultural Affairs.

Careers in Dance

For one of the most realistic overviews of dance, catch a performance of Michael Bennett's history-making musical, *A Chorus Line,* about a diverse group of performers auditioning for the chorus of a Broadway show. It gives a timeless perspective on the hope, drive, and disappointment these relentless hoofers experience. At the same time, poignant individuals emerge from their painstakingly hopeful anonymity.

Dancers are placed in numerous categories, such as classical ballet, modern, tap, jazz, ballroom, and ethnic. Each area demands different methods of study and levels of endurance. Solo ballet and modern performers and ensemble members are most often affiliated with a specific dance company. If you are a staunch individualist, performing as a guest artist with various troupes or freelancing wherever work becomes available might be a good idea. However, to make the proper connections and attain recognition, company affiliation is obligatory before you decide to go it alone.

Disciplines naturally overlap in dance, a profession that requires intense hands-on training passed down through the generations by accomplished artists. Choreographers are also dancers, so they understand how a dancer's body moves. They create original dances—either short pieces or full-length ballets—or restage classics such as *The Nutcracker* or *Swan Lake*. Sometimes they prefer to work with specific dancers around whose unique abilities they develop a dance. Completing a work, then auditioning dancers for that piece, is another option. They rehearse for long, odd hours.

Artistic directors are in charge of programming and the overall running of a dance company, while managing directors oversee the group's finances. Both are positions appointed by a board of directors, which also has the authority to retain or fire its administrative choices.

A ballet master (or ballet mistress) is a professional classical dancer who is an effective teacher familiar with a company's repertoire. He or she restages ballets and coaches lead dancers.

Careers in Music

The music field is incredibly expansive, with styles ranging from classical and Klezmer to show tunes, pop, rock, jazz, blues, soul, folk, reggae, rap, country, ska, and fusions of all of the above. In general terms, musicians may play instruments, sing, compose, arrange, or conduct groups in instrumental or vocal performances.

Singers interpret music with special attention to melody and harmony. They are classified according to their vocal range: soprano, contralto, tenor, baritone, or bass. Style also serves to place them in music's endless subcategories.

A burgeoning arena is that of composing music and writing lyrics—running the gamut of symphonies, operas, musicals, popular songs, and commercial jingles. A deep sensitivity to sound is essential, along with a comprehensive understanding of many instruments and how they interact.

Conductors and concertmasters work together in leading their orchestras or bands, auditioning musicians, and determining programming. A conductor is schooled in a complex kind of sign language that his or her players decipher in order to achieve the best possible unified sound.

Choral directors are similar to conductors, except they guide voices instead of instruments. They play a major role in operas and classical concerts that demand authentic choral mastery.

Careers in Opera

The "Three Tenors"—Luciano Pavarotti, Placido Domingo, and José Carreras—and their spinoffs, such as Three Mo' Tenors and the Three Irish Tenors, are greatly responsible for bringing opera to the masses today. Although Europe's opera tradition is part of the fabric of its culture, America has fostered a more limited, specific opera audience. There are the purists, of course, who only consider works performed in their original language and setting to be acceptable. Others favor experimental new works in English. Then there's an entire contingent of Gilbert and Sullivan operetta buffs.

Whatever operatic style you choose to pursue, realize that this field does not have as many diva-esque positions available as you may think. There are not too many Jessye Normans or Cecilia

Bartolis warbling to Wagner's Norse gods. But job openings in opera choruses are numerous. This is a highly competitive arena that demands total mastery and control of one's voice, breathing, foreign language skills, characterization, and stage presence. Unlike heavily nuanced contemporary theatre, opera is still a powerful proponent of the grand gesture.

However, more theatre directors have been asked to stage operas, resulting in more contemporary takes on the classics. British director Richard Jones staged Humperdinck's *Hansel and Gretel* with a wry nod to Hannibal Lecter, and American director Diane Paulus transported Monteverdi's *Orfeo* to a swank cocktail party. One of the latest operas to open in New York City is based on the "Jerry Springer Show."

Musical directors in opera are the equivalent of directors in theatre. They have many of the same coordinating and interpreting duties, in addition to holding auditions and leading rehearsals. Like their singers, they must be very involved in the language and style of the work they are presenting. Pulling it all together are the accompanist and the prompter. The former accompanies the singers on piano during rehearsals and vocal coaching sessions, and the latter gives the performers music cues from a little box under the front portion of the stage.

Careers in Theatrical Design

Designers are truly the unsung heroes and heroines of the performing arts. We enjoy their props, costumes, and lighting designs, but all too frequently we forget that their work is as critical to the success of a performance as the actors' emoting on stage. Specialized curriculums are available across the country for theatrical designers, which include scenery and properties, lighting, sound, and costume professionals. Theatrical designers consult with directors, producers, and cast on the viability of their ideas. Other related occupations are properties masters, who make sure props are in their correct places on stage, and backstage dressers, who are responsible for getting the actors in and out of their costumes at lightning speed.

Teaching Opportunities in the Performing Arts

As discussed earlier, skills in the performing arts are passed on from experienced mentors to students. Therefore, educators are also actors, directors, dancers, musicians, opera singers, and designers. Many arts instructors teach in high schools and universities while remaining active on the stage. They also conduct seminars, workshops, and master classes in many specialized art forms.

Careers in Arts Writing and Publicity

Arts writers, critics, and publicists work hand in hand as they constantly exchange information about openings, guest artists, arts news, and feature leads. Publicists, who represent an artist or a company, create media packets and then follow through with calls to targeted members of this niche press market. The field of writing and criticism is greatly in need of journalists who have a strong understanding of and/or experience in the arts. They must be engaged in the same fervent manner as the artists. In major theatre cities, like New York and Chicago, an enclave of established critics exists—and rarely do they leave their coveted positions.

Some are on the staffs of major newspapers, but the majority are freelance writers who work for multiple publications. The Internet has created even more opportunities for wide-reaching writing outlets devoted to arts coverage. Magazines and newspapers typically have corresponding websites.

Performing Arts and the Internet

Peforming arts directories have exploded on the Internet. A massive array of arts organizations from around the world now have websites. Online audition bulletins and artists' head shots and resumes are extremely popular. Some of the oft-repeated categories on Google.com include Audition Online, Casting Online, Casting Source, Talent Bank International, the Talent Network, and Theatre Jobs Online.

Interactive programs are already following suit. If your computer is equipped with CD-ROM and other audio capabilities, you can download dance—and other arts-related—performances. Cyberspace is creating a whole new stage for performers, where they can act, dance, write, compose, and design for computer-only entertainment.

Sign on and get those search engines, or Web browsers, activated. An enlightening place to start is the International Society for the Performing Arts' homepage (www.ispa.org). Here's some of what you'll learn.

Founded in 1949, the International Society for the Performing Arts (ISPA) Foundation is a not-for-profit international organization of more than six hundred executives and directors of concert and performance halls, festivals, performing companies, and artist competitions; government cultural officials; artists' managers; and other performing arts professionals in more than fifty countries.

The purpose of ISPA is to develop, nurture, energize, and educate an international network of arts leaders and professionals who are dedicated to advancing the field of the performing arts. ISPA and its membership are committed to:

- increasing international communication, understanding, and cooperation among all arts professionals through its programs, meetings and services
- strengthening the leadership capabilities of member arts institutions
- providing support to enrich creative potential and intellectual growth in the field
- affirming the importance and necessity of the performing arts in today's society

As an organization, ISPA's constant goal is to provide the best possible support, information, and opportunities for collegial exchange to members throughout the world.

··

For More Information

Publications

Bureau of Labor Statistics, U.S. Department of Labor, *Occupational Outlook Handbook,* 2002–2003 Edition (www.bls.gov).

Chronicle Guidance Briefs, Vol. 2, Career Information Center, Glencoe/MacMillan.

Encyclopedia of Careers and Vocational Guidance, Eighth Edition, Ferguson Publishing Company.

Stern's Performing Arts Directory, 33 West Sixtieth Street, Tenth Floor, New York, NY 10023.

Theatre Associations

American Alliance for Theatre and Education
Department of Theatre
Arizona State University
Box 873411
Tempe, AZ 85287
www.aate.com

Americans for the Arts
One East Fifty-Third Street
New York, NY 10022
www.artsusa.org

American Symphony Orchestra League
910 Seventeenth Street NW
Washington, DC 20006
www.symphony.org

National Association of Schools of Theatre
11250 Roger Bacon Drive, Suite 21
Reston, VA 20190
www.arts-accredit.org

Theatre Communications Group
520 Eighth Avenue, Twenty-Fourth Floor
New York, NY 10018
www.tcg.org

Dance Associations

American Alliance for Health, Physical Education, Recreation
and Dance
1900 Association Drive
Reston, VA 20191
www.aahperd.org

National Association of Schools of Dance
11250 Roger Bacon Drive, Suite 21
Reston, VA 20190
www.arts-accredit.org

American Dance Guild
P.O. Box 2006
Lennox Hill Station
New York, NY 10021
www.americandanceguild.org

Society of Stage Directors and Choreographers
1501 Broadway, Suite 1701
New York, NY 10036
www.ssdc.org

Dance/USA
1156 Fifteenth Street NW, Suite 820
Washington, DC 20005
www.danceusa.org

Music Associations

National Association of Schools of Music
11250 Roger Bacon Drive, Suite 21
Reston, VA 20190
www.arts-accredit.org

Chamber Music America
305 Seventh Avenue, Fifth Floor
New York, NY 10001
www.chamber-music.org

American Guild of Organists
475 Riverside Drive, Suite 1260
New York, NY 10115
www.agohq.org

Opera America
1156 Fifteenth Street NW, Suite 810
Washington, DC 20005
www.operaam.org

Other Associations

National Association of Schools of Art and Design
11250 Roger Bacon Drive, Suite 21
Reston, VA 20190
www.arts-accredit.org

National Art Education Association
1916 Association Drive
Reston, VA 20190
www.naea-reston.org

National Foundation for Advancement in the Arts
800 Brickell Avenue, Suite 500
Miami, FL 33131
www.nfaa.org

CHAPTER TWO

Careers in Theatre

I f you feel energized, instead of terrified, about speaking or performing before a large group of people, read on. A career in theatre could be the answer. A high percentage of actors say they were inspired by seeing a live show that enthralled them. Or they enjoyed being the center of attention—putting on shows in their parents' living room or getting cast in school plays.

Although some of these outgoing individuals outgrow the fantasy of portraying other characters, a large contingent of dedicated actors make it their lives. And if they are committed to their craft, meticulous, and willing to improve, they only get better with age. Even Laurence Olivier did not consider his early portrayal of Shakespeare's indomitable King Lear to be convincing. Through his own tempestuous life experiences, the legendary English actor truly learned how to play Lear at the age of seventy-five.

That's not to say all great actors must lead equally dramatic private lives. They just should be more keenly aware of applying those life experiences to their roles on stage. Ultimately, high energy and a balanced temperament will help you, as an actor, keep things in perspective.

Directors, producers, and stage managers can be viewed as the behind-the-scenes string pullers (dramatic and financial). They are all involved in ensuring that a production runs smoothly, is fiscally sound, and conveys their unique vision. Without them, actors would have no guidance on stage.

And without playwrights, no one would have anything to perform. Writers are responsible for our most rewarding theatrical experiences. Imagine life without Shakespeare, Anton Chekhov,

Tennessee Williams, Lillian Hellman, August Wilson, Tony Kushner, or the countless others who have crafted poignant scenes with expertly chiseled words and moving phrases. Living playwrights can be involved directly in staging a production. Their talent and marketing skills earn them recognition, especially if they move in key theatrical circles. Through university programs, beginning playwrights also have a chance to present their work.

Dramaturgs, or historians, typically hold advanced degrees in English literature, language and linguistics, history, or theatre. They are well versed in the specialized language of theatre and understand the close connection between literature and the stage. Such a position, however, is not in tremendous demand. Many dramaturgs are also university instructors.

Puppeteers, like visual artists, learn their trade through apprenticeships with skilled craftspeople. Additionally, they have the same training as actors, with the advanced specialization of manipulating mechanical figures called puppets. They, too, often hold other jobs in theatre besides puppetry.

Actors

Being a successful actor involves more than just memorizing and reciting lines. To feel a role and draw from your own experiences in the interpretive process are vital requirements for enabling an audience to become immersed in a production. You must also establish your relationship with the other characters and be willing to do in-depth research before you even begin rehearsals.

There is no getting around the rigorous training and hectic schedules of an actor's life. No sooner do you get cast, rehearse twelve hours a day, and perform between six and ten shows a week than you already have to start keeping your eyes and ears open for upcoming auditions—not to mention polishing your technique, taking extra classes, and keeping your head shots and resumes up-to-date.

Since rehearsals usually run in the afternoon and evening—and actors perform until late at night—you should work out a schedule that allows you to rest in the morning, study your part, and hold a day job. Ask actors about their choice of employment to pay the rent and, nine times out of ten, they will tell you they "temp." That is, they work as temporary employees in offices, warehouses, art studios, telemarketing companies, and elsewhere. It's flexible, undemanding, and most firms tend to be understanding about actors' audition and rehearsal schedules.

If your ideas do not seem to coincide with the theatrical offerings in your area, you might consider starting your own company or getting into performance art. Most performance artists are poets who collaborate with other artists on off-beat projects. They build a following and tout their experimental ideas at coffeehouses and alternative clubs.

Mime, a profession ripe for ridicule, is frequently incorporated into avant-garde performances. Most recognizable as white-faced street entertainers, mimes have made great—albeit silent—strides in American theatre. Multimedia mime and dance companies are a growing trend, and mime schools (which also teach circus arts and traditional acting) exist across the country.

If you can think on the spot, improvisation is a specialized area of theatre that allows you to create a script on stage based on audience suggestions or interaction among the actors. Using a variety of free-association techniques, you can develop a play immediately, right in front of the audience. Many improv troupes have been cropping up in major U.S. theatre cities. They employ a diverse range of methods, such as long-form improv, literary-based parodies, fully improvised musicals, and loosely scripted shows that rely on audience recommendations to further the action or toss in plot twists.

Whatever area you choose, be assured that acting is an all-encompassing art form. Its subcategories ultimately create a unified whole.

Getting Started

Acting is one of those open areas of the performing arts with no limits on age. You can be three years old or ninety years old (or anywhere in between), depending on what type of character is needed. Some actors don't begin their careers until midlife, while child performers may move into a nonarts career as adults. So, with a variety of options available, you can basically pursue acting anytime. The late Jessica Tandy worked right up to her last days.

School plays and community theatre afford endless performing opportunities for individuals wishing to hone their skills and get constructive criticism. Even if you do not feel ready to make your debut, go to auditions anyway as an invaluable form of research. Observe other actors and get a sense of what qualities directors are seeking in an actor.

Being a regular audience member at live theatrical events can only help you better understand the overall workings of the stage. Visit bookstores that specialize in scripts. Read a variety of plays (comedies, dramas, musicals, Shakespearean works, histories) and practice the various styles of dialogue to get a feel for the rhythms of speech. Keep up with theatre reviews and read the arts sections of newspapers and magazines. The more you immerse yourself in the field, the better prepared you will be to step confidently into the spotlight.

Educational and Apprenticeship Requirements

Formal dramatic training and acting experience are necessary to break into acting. Of course, there are those rare individuals who hit it big without ever having taken a scene study course or a voice lesson. But, for the most part, a solid, well-rounded education is needed. Colleges and universities across the United States offer fully accredited degree programs in each separate area of theatre.

No doubt, New York offers prolific opportunities for study and performance opportunities. But there are stellar theatrical study programs available everywhere. Many of them offer overseas internships, such as summers spent working with the Royal Shakespeare Company in London.

College drama curricula usually include courses in liberal arts, acting, characterization, monologue, stage speech and movement, directing, playwriting, production, design, and theatre history. Actors need talent, creative ability, and training that enable them to portray a gamut of characters. Training in singing and dancing is especially useful. Actors must have poise, stage presence, and the ability to affect an audience and to follow directions.

A closer look at several programs will give you a feel for the specific types of courses offered: Abraham Lincoln High Academic, Visual and Performing Arts Magnet School in San Jose, California; Emerson College of Performing Arts in Boston, Massachusetts; and Ithaca College School of Humanities and Sciences in Ithaca, New York.

Lincoln High School: Academic, Visual and Performing Arts Magnet. The drama classes at Lincoln focus on performance, and every student participates in theatre production. Technical theatre students design sets and lighting for school productions and are also hired to run productions for West Valley Light Opera, Opera San José, and Children's Musical Theater. Students perform for San Jose Repertory Theatre, Theatre Under the Stars, and other professional groups, while the Drama Tour Group attends productions in North America and Europe.

Beginning, intermediate, and advanced drama students at Lincoln concentrate on acting and theatre technique, vocabulary, improvisation, and a survey of theatre history. There is extensive scene and monologue work, as well as an introduction to improvisation. Lincoln is one of the few schools in the Bay Area to feature the concept of "Comedy Sports" in the classroom, which develops focus, concentration, and awareness on stage. Advanced students explore the history of theatre by reading, rehearsing, and videotaping a performance of a different play each month. Each class selects, stages, designs, and presents one or more one-act plays in a public performance. Every student in class participates on stage or as the director.

The Drama Tour Group is a class chosen by student audition. Sixteen students are selected to form a performing group to represent Lincoln at local schools, community events, and competitions. The focus of the class is on performance and preparation of audition material for scholarship, community, and professional auditions.

The Technical Theatre class is responsible for the scenery, lighting, sound, and direction of all Lincoln productions. In addition to learning basic stagecraft and proper procedures, the students are given the opportunity to work with a computerized lighting system and wireless microphones. Many technical theatre students are hired by community and professional companies to run their productions throughout the Bay Area.

The Theatre Performance class affords students selected by audition to produce Broadway musicals and plays for the entire school's enjoyment. The students rehearse for six to twelve weeks, learning to develop characters and to refine acting, singing, dancing, and makeup skills. Many Lincoln students go on to perform with the American Musical Theatre of San Jose, San Jose Rep, West Valley Light Opera, national tours, and even on Broadway.

The Musical Theater class offers music students the opportunity to perform on stage in Broadway musicals and plays in conjunction with the Drama and Dance departments.

Emerson College. Emerson College in Boston, Massachusetts, boasts one of the largest professionally focused theatre and dance programs in the country, with diversity among faculty and curricular options. Emerson Performing Arts offers a complete education through very focused theatre studies, which are more extensive than narrow skills training. At the same time, the program enables students to develop expertise in clearly defined specialty areas. The curriculum combines intensive studio and laboratory and production experiences with a broad study of the history of the physical theatre and of dramatic literature, including Asian, South American, and African theatre. Emerson's liberal arts core anchors the professional training program. This combination provides students with the opportunity to learn and grow as individuals and as artists.

Concentrations include acting, musical theatre, dance, design and technology, production and management, theatre education, and theatre studies. Admission to Emerson as a performing arts major is based on academic qualifications and an audition or portfolio review.

Emerson Stage provides all performing arts students with extensive opportunities to apply and develop skills by contributing to student and professional productions. Each year, many projects are fully mounted or shared as workshops, and a variety of other student-directed projects are produced. Guest designers, actors, and directors act as mentors to students who work with them, as do faculty and the professional staffs of the fully equipped scene and costume shops.

The Majestic Theatre, Emerson's main performance space, is located in the heart of Boston's theatre district. Professionally staged performances enable students to work with the American Repertory Theatre and other professional organizations.

The Brimmer Street Theatre serves as a second major performance space, housing a variety of productions. Three other performance spaces serve various productions directed, acted, staffed, and often written by students throughout the year.

The Musical Theatre Society participates in musical productions both on and off campus and sponsors guest appearances by leading musical theatre personalities. Each spring the society coproduces a major musical in association with Emerson Stage.

Several comedy groups provide a forum for students to perform or have their material performed in workshop settings. Each year, Emerson Stage produces an Emerson Comedy Showcase.

The Emerson Dance Company welcomes both the accomplished and the beginning dancer to take part in company efforts in performance and choreography.

Performing arts students are encouraged to study at Emerson's satellite campuses. For example, second-year acting students can work under the leadership of professional actor/teachers from the Netherlands. Semester programs in Los Angeles allow students to study acting, design and technology, and production and management with professionals who understand the demands of film and television work. Internships are also supported and encouraged.

Ithaca College. Majoring in theatre arts at Ithaca is a rigorous experience. Students may major in one of the department's performance-based B.F.A. programs in acting, musical theatre, or theatrical production arts (with concentrations in theatrical design or theatre technology); the liberal arts–based B.A. program in drama; or the B.S. program in theatre arts management. All majors have unique opportunities to act, dance, design, build, direct, and manage as part of the department's active season of faculty- and student-directed productions. The department's theatre, music, dance, and opera performances draw large community audiences and are staged in one of two superb theatres housed in the Dillingham Center for the Performing Arts.

The department offers specialized instruction in all major areas, yet it is small enough to allow the quality of individualized instruction that the arts require. Approximately eighty courses are offered in the following areas:

- Stagecraft
- Stage lighting
- Scene design
- Directing
- Theatre organization and management
- Daytime television drama production

- Dance for the musical stage
- Professional internship

Continuing Education for Actors

The following information is reprinted, with permission, from an article written by the author that appeared in *PerformInk*, a Chicago-based performing arts trade publication.

....

It's basically a given that musicians, dancers, vocalists, and athletes adhere to an ongoing rigorous training regimen. But what about actors? When they are not in a show, do they continually hone their craft and fine-tune their entire being? According to a varied group of local coaches and actors, the standard answer is "Not as often as they should," followed by solid arguments in favor of consistent training.

One of the latest buzz phrases is "educating the whole body" as theatre moves more vigorously into a physical arena.

"Actors must be committed to a character right down to their toes," says Michael Menendian, private monologue and scene study coach and Raven Theatre's artistic director. "Often their speech patterns are saying one thing and their body is saying something different."

Movement classes have been on the rise to help performers become more comfortable with their entire instrument on the stage. Just take a look at most of the fall brochures from the city's training centers, and you'll see that courses involving exercise and various forms of stylized movement are as numerous as the scene study offerings.

"We emphasize physical concentration, not acting from the neck up," explains Tony Adler, cofounder and codirector of the Actors Gymnasium in Evanston, Illinois. "Many of the physically demanding techniques taught today are a reaction against a purely mental form of training that had been going on for years."

Affiliated with the Lookingglass Theatre, the Actors Gymnasium understandably works with actors interested in expanding their performance abilities. A course titled Text and the Body is a fitting example of the center's athletic focus. It's described as "a wildly physical approach to the energy of stage language, pushing the sounds and words of a theatrical text through physical principles borrowed from modern dance, movement improv, gymnastics, and wrestling."

As more demands are placed on actors, ongoing study may become mandatory. It's certainly a step in the right direction for individuals who plan on devoting their lives to such a tenuous, competitive, and unpredictable profession.

"We have a wide assortment of actors," says Kate Buckley, who teaches folio technique together with Bob Scogin. "Some come in to rehearse a specific audition piece, while others return to sharpen their skills.

"Actors' training should be constant. If it's not, the muscles get weak."

She adds that important areas for performers to work on are physical movement (knowing your body better), vocal training, projection, articulation, and "finding the character's voice—their center—so that it's clear and true."

When she lectures around the country, Buckley dubs her folio technique "Shakespeare without fear." Put together by the actors in Shakespeare's original company, the folio is considered closest to the Bard's text. Commenting on the small size of most Chicago theatres, Buckley observes that actors are not used to projecting when called upon to play a larger venue.

"This is something we concentrate on in our training sessions," she continues. "Actors can only recite so many monologues in their bathroom, living room, or on small stages before diminishing their capacity for projecting."

On the physical side, Courtney Brown—a fully certified teacher of the hundred-year-old Alexander Technique—helps actors eliminate bad postural habits, which can affect breathing, voice, and projection. This method makes no distinction between mind and body and focuses on improved means of working the head, neck, and back.

"My goal is not so much to teach new things as to retrain actors who might suddenly be tensing, for example," notes Brown. "Tension is not fully under one's conscious control. So we want to get the motor area working and allow actors to learn how to feel what's wrong. We awaken a greater kinesthetic awareness in them."

Actors at all levels are advised never to stop learning—even if they are caught up in a whirlwind of shows.

"Scheduling conflicts can make it difficult for actors to take regular classes, and I believe one of the best classrooms is working on a show," comments Ruth Farrimond, [former] artistic director of Frump Tucker Theatre Company. "But when time permits, actors should really focus on audition, monologue, movement, and improv classes."

Improv, in fact, has become a common form of drilling theatre artists in characterization. It allows for a loose kind of exploration of a role or situation with benefits that extend to various acting styles. Mark Gagné, [former] artistic director of the Free Associates (known for their fully improvised literary adaptations), encourages both traditional actors and improvisers to balance improv classes with performing in order to keep their skills fresh.

"It's like a psychic sense," says Gagné. "You can lose your intuitive skills as an ensemble if you stop working at your craft."

He cited two schools of thought regarding improv polishing: one claiming that spontaneity gets lost if you rehearse too much, and the other, which regards a balanced style of rehearsing and performing as an effective way to master and maintain quickness and creativity. Gagné favors the latter approach.

Menendian, who coaches actors one-on-one or two-on-one in monologue development and cold reading, finds that many of his students are fairly established and have theatre-related degrees but are frustrated with their audition materials.

"We clean up the old material or start from scratch and develop new material," he says. "I concentrate on my own version of method acting that involves a full psychological, emotional, and physical commitment to a role. After all, we are students of the human condition.

"Most importantly, I stress focus and total immersion. In auditions, actors have a tendency to worry about being judged—about external circumstances beyond their control instead of working the mind and body 100 percent, dissecting a character, and making unpredictable choices."

"Monologue Mom" Belinda Bremner grows adamant when discussing the importance of outside perspective for audition pieces: "You can't do an audition piece without having a professional take a look at it—I don't care if you're Olivier."

An expert monologue and dialect coach, Bremner believes that when actors go on for years doing what they think works for them, they forget some of those steps that got them to a certain point. Work can soon grow stale.

"You absolutely need fresh audition pieces," she emphasizes. "That shows the theatre community that you haven't been sitting on your duff. I can't stress enough the need to get constant feedback and be well prepared."

Bremner also finds that actors wait until the last minute to acquire precision-perfect dialect skills. It may take an audition for a Sean O'Casey festival or a role in a Eugene O'Neill play to prompt them to focus on an accent that should already have been in place.

"I tell my students to learn the dialect before learning the lines," she adds. "It's crucial to know what has influenced that speech pattern—what's the background of the culture. Everyone needs to master British, Irish, standard working class, various American dialects, and clean American speech."

When it comes to film actors, Bob Mohler focuses on improv technique ("the best friend of film") in his audition classes and immersion in his on-camera and on-location sessions. A working film and stage actor and founder of Eclipse Theatre Company, Mohler conducts these ongoing, time-limitless classes to give actors an opportunity to "establish their beyond."

"In film, rarely does a director tell you exactly what to do," he explains. "Sometimes they don't give you any direction at all. So it's up to the actors to establish where their characters came from, what they were doing before the scene, where they're going.

"When you're delivering a monologue, you have to be able to convey that you really are looking out at the ocean or feeling the air. That can only come about by propelling yourself into a constant routine of study and practice."

On a cautionary note, Greg Kolack—co-artistic director of Circle Theatre—recommends that actors sufficiently check out classes and workshops and make sure they will meet their needs. He also would like to see more courses on the business side of theatre.

"It's important for actors to sign up for classes with the intention of improving," says Kolack. "If they just sign up for something in order to get noticed—and later cast—by the famous director who's teaching it, they will be gravely disappointed."

As proof that even long-established celebrities need to brush up on their skills, television and film actor Tony Danza admits: "I take my acting very seriously—it's not willy-nilly. As intuitive as acting may be for me, I still have to prepare. I continue to study voice, speech, piano, you name it. It's when you stop learning that you become complacent."

That only reinforces director Kay Martinovich's theory that "it takes a lifetime to be a great actor."

How to Find Jobs in Theatre

Theatre is a very visual occupation. So the best way to find a job is by being consistently seen throughout the theatre community. Attending auditions, performing, and/or working behind the scenes will help move your career forward. As a supplement to your stage work, register with reputable talent agencies, which can pass your head shots and resumes along to casting agents for commercials, print ads, or training videos. Not only is this extra income, it shows theatre professionals that you have diverse experience.

As an actor, don't be afraid to cultivate different "looks" as a way of showing the range of characters or types you can portray. As the reputations of actors, directors, producers, playwrights, and other theatre artists grow, opportunities to work on larger productions or in more prestigious theatres expand. Actors also advance to lead or specialized roles. Some actors move into acting-related jobs as drama coaches of stage, television, radio, or motion picture productions. Others teach drama on the university level.

The length of a performer's working life depends largely on training, skill, versatility, and perseverance. Those fortunate enough to get consistent work stay on in the profession. But there also exists a high number of performers who only last a short time in the business because they can't find enough substantial work to make a living—or the work they do get doesn't quite pay the rent.

Directors, Producers, and Stage Managers

Directors have a variety of options. They can work on a freelance basis, submitting scripts and ideas to theatrical companies. Some choose to work in residence for a troupe, while others found their own theatre companies with specific goals in mind. But they all essentially have the same responsibility: to guide an ensemble of actors in a play that reflects a distinct interpretation.

Directors audition and select cast members, conduct rehearsals, and oversee the entire process—from actors, dancers, and musicians to designers and box office staff. Directors come from acting backgrounds, so they speak the profession's language. Using their knowledge of acting, voice, and movement, they aim to elicit the best possible performance from the team of actors and designers.

It's possible for someone to produce and direct a show, but for purposes of clarity, we list a separate definition for each position. Producers are the entrepreneurial arm of the business. They select plays or scripts, arrange financing, and decide on the size and content of the production and its budget. They also hire directors, principal cast members, and key production staff members.

Negotiating contracts with artistic personnel—often in accordance with collective bargaining agreements—is a major responsibility. Producers coordinate the activities of writers, directors, managers, and other personnel. Both directors and producers frequently work under stress as they try to meet schedules, stay within budgets, and resolve personnel problems while putting together a production.

Stage managers are the "invisible organizers" who assist directors with daily rehearsals and make sure the actors get on and off the stage at the proper times. They, too, work long, irregular hours and are essential for the smooth running of a show.

Getting Started

Directors, producers, and stage managers have most likely performed on stage at some point in their lives. They therefore start out in much the same way actors do. The main difference: they are more comfortable managing a production and working behind the scenes. One director commented that he chose his profession when he realized he would rather take on the "angst of all the characters in a play" than concentrate on the interpretation of one as an actor.

If you like to look at the big picture and have a definitive vision of the finished product, directing is something you could begin practicing in high school. By working alongside your drama teacher, who is in charge of directing the annual musical, for instance, you can participate in the evolution of a show. You will learn organizational, interpretative, and instructional skills. A good director is not a dictator. You must be able to balance your set ideas with those of the cast members. Stage managers also get extensive hands-on experience through school and community theatre productions.

Producers should be well versed in all of the above. However, they have to come in with a solid grasp of business procedures. They make the numbers happen. Working part-time in a theatre box office would give you a glimpse at how money is managed. Later, aim to pursue a degree in finance and arts management or arts administration.

Educational and Apprenticeship Requirements

There are no specific training requirements for directors, producers, and stage managers. However, talent, experience, and business acumen are very important. Degrees in directing, acting, or scenic design are useful. For the most part, directors and producers come from different backgrounds. Actors, writers, and business managers often enter these fields. Producers traditionally start in the industry working behind the scenes with successful directors.

Playwrights

Today, especially through universities and dramatist workshops, playwrights have more outlets to test their work than they did decades ago when the field was not so open or well defined. Most academic programs include separate playwriting courses for majors and minors. If you are inclined to write for the stage, there is also the possibility of hooking up with a resident theatrical group for which you can create plays directly. Like writers in other genres, playwrights benefit from having an agent who can market their work to key decision makers.

Getting Started

Talent for the written word often comes from within. So it's not surprising that most writers begin putting pen to paper (or fingers to computer keyboard) at an early age. They polish these skills in the classroom, typically excelling in creative writing and English courses. Excessive reading comes with the territory. And, if you opt to write for the theatre, attending performances regularly is a must. Spend time at theatres to observe trends and check out the competition.

By observing the way actors speak and move about the stage, you become familiar with a whole new way of constructing a story. Practice this specialized genre by assigning yourself fun, enlightening exercises. Take certain passages from a novel and try turning them into dialogue for the stage. Or mentally put two people in a room together and let them talk while you write.

Your teachers and guidance counselors are great resources for outstanding college playwriting programs. They can also inform you about writing contests and workshops. Most importantly, get started by writing—essays, short stories, poems, letters, and stream-of-consciousness ponderings. Maintaining a daily or weekly journal will keep you focused and in touch with your feelings, as well as help you determine subjects or issues closest to your heart.

When you are ready, ask professionals to read your scripts and give you constructive criticism. Participate in staged readings with post-show discussion groups for more vital feedback. Create a lifestyle for yourself that allows you to meet your goal of writing a designated number of words per day. Stay in touch with local theatrical troupes interested in producing original works.

Educational and Apprenticeship Requirements

Playwriting has quite a prominent place in college theatre curricula. Specific courses are available through most theatre departments. But because many playwrights write in other genres, too, they traditionally major in English or writing. Master's or doctoral degrees are not necessary as long as the playwright has talent, skills, and a solid educational foundation, along with the determination and confidence to network with key industry players.

Dramaturgs/Historians

These experts in the re-creation of dramatic works act as consultants to the director, designers, and cast. They have in-depth knowledge of historic periods, language, literature, speech patterns, and cues. Dramaturgs and historians provide knowledge essential to presenting an accurate staging. They work closely with playwrights and production teams, but they do not always have to endure the long, rigorous rehearsals or be present at all performances. Because positions as dramaturgs are not plentiful, holding another job is common.

Getting Started

Dramaturgs, or theatre historians, are similar to playwrights in that they are attracted to liberal arts courses and the theatre. Rarely will a high school student say, "I want to become a dramaturg when I grow up." This is the kind of occupation that evolves as the result of pursuing a theatrical history or linguistic education.

Getting started generally involves studying history and English while being an active theatre supporter. Attend plays and even seek out backstage jobs. This way, you can get a keen sense of how theatres operate and how the script properly connects to its historic backdrop. Make yourself a fixture at area museums, where you can observe firsthand the remnants of world history.

Educational and Apprenticeship Requirements

Dramaturgs and historians follow a standard liberal arts curriculum, with emphasis on theatre, literature, rhetoric, linguistics, and world history. They are experts in their fields and often hold master's and doctoral degrees. In addition to working with theatre companies, they teach and write books, treatises, and scholarly journal articles.

Puppeteers

Puppetry is an ancient art form that continues to gain popularity in mainstream theatre. But unless you have established your own puppet troupe, work in this specialized field remains sporadic. On the other hand, a number of adventurous theatre companies incorporate puppetry into their productions, and entire plays are performed by life-size "puppet" casts. Teaming up with seasoned puppeteers is the best way to hone your skills.

Getting Started

Children's theatre is a logical place to start learning the fundamentals of puppetry. Granted, the present era promotes puppet versions of classic plays geared toward adults. But those productions involve a wide array of mechanical devices, life-size puppets, and complicated masks, props, and scenery. It's a good idea to begin on a much smaller scale. Most theatre companies and acting centers offer classes in puppetry. Or you might want to volunteer at children's theatre programs through your local park district or community acting troupe.

Familiarize yourself with the tools of the trade. Many contemporary puppets are soft sculptures (fabric, stuffing, and paint), while others are made of a variety of materials—wood, molded plastic, clay, and papier-mâché.

If you happen to be in Europe, which has a long, rich puppet tradition, inquire about marionette museums for a fascinating overview of the profession. One of the largest puppet museums is in Palermo, Sicily. Called the International Museum of Marionettes, it showcases the classic puppet styles of Italy as well as the shadow puppets of Asia and life-size contemporary constructions.

A comprehensive video presentation traces the progression of puppets over the centuries. On display are elaborately decorated puppets reenacting the romances of Charlemagne, Rinaldo, and Orlando Furioso. Mythological figures, such as sirens, devils, birds, skeletons, and centaurs, hover over Saracen invaders. Many marionettes are equipped with heads and limbs that can be "severed" at the deft twist of a wire. Mazelike rooms contain shimmering gold Chinese dragon chariots, Japanese Bunraku (full-body, self-walking) styles, original commedia dell'arte figures, and the full mechanical cast of Rossini's *The Barber of Seville.*

UNIMA, the international organization of puppeteers, is an excellent source of information. It hosts annual competitions around the world for the most poignantly crafted puppet productions. Its UNIMA-USA Award is the highest honor bestowed by its American branch.

Begun in September 1978, the Center for Puppetry Arts in Atlanta, Georgia, is the largest institution in the United States dedicated to the art form of puppetry and focuses on three areas: performance, museum, and education. Housed in a former school building, the three-story center includes two theatres, a special exhibit gallery, rehearsal space, library, workshop rooms, multipurpose room, and gift shop.

The center's museum program provides visitors with a basic understanding of the puppetry performance process. The education program offers workshops and classes for children and adults, including special programs for teachers and persons with disabilities.

Educational and Apprenticeship Requirements

There are no degrees available in puppetry. Therefore, puppet artists receive the bulk of their training from seasoned puppeteers and craftspeople. They join a troupe and work alongside mentors, learning to build puppets out of wood, plastic, papier-mâché, cloth, and other materials and to add the mechanical elements and manipulate the figures in order to make them look and sound lifelike. Acting classes provide the necessary stage skills to activate the puppets and eventually free yourself from the constraints of the human scale and form.

Salary and Success Outlook for Theatre Artists

It is difficult to discuss a standard fee for all performers, since work is sporadic and based on a number of conditions. For the most part, however, minimum salaries, hours of work, and other conditions of employment are covered in collective bargaining agreements between producers of shows and unions representing workers in this field.

The Actors Equity Association represents stage actors; the Screen Actors Guild (SAG) covers actors in motion pictures, including television, commercials, and films; and the American Federation of Television and Radio Artists (AFTRA) represents television and radio performers. Most stage directors belong to the Society of Stage Directors and Choreographers, and film and television directors belong to the Directors Guild of America. Please note that any actor or director may negotiate for a salary higher than the minimum.

On July 1, 2001, the members of SAG and AFTRA negotiated a new joint contract covering all unionized employment. Under the contract, motion picture and television actors with speaking parts earned a minimum daily rate of $636 or $2,206 for a five-day week. Actors also receive contributions to their health and pension plans and additional compensation for reruns and foreign telecasts of the productions in which they appear.

According to Actors Equity, the minimum weekly salary for actors in Broadway productions as of 2001 was $1,252. Those in small "off-Broadway" theatres received minimums ranging from $440 to $551 a week, depending on the seating capacity of the theatre. Regional theatres that operate under an Equity agreement paid actors $500 to $728 per week. For touring shows, actors received an additional $106 per day for living expenses.

Actors usually work long hours during rehearsals. Once the show opens, they have more regular hours, working about thirty hours a week. Earnings from acting are low because employment is so irregular. The Screen Actors Guild also reports that the average income its members earned from acting was less than $5,000 a year. Therefore, many actors must supplement their incomes by holding jobs in other fields.

Some well-known actors have salary rates well above the minimums, and the salaries of the few top stars are many times the figures cited, creating a false impression that all actors are highly paid.

Many actors who work more than a set number of weeks per year are covered by a union health, welfare, and pension fund, including hospitalization insurance, to which employers contribute. Under some employment conditions, Actors Equity and AFTRA members receive paid vacations and sick leave.

Earnings of stage directors vary greatly. Median annual earnings of producers and directors were $41,030 in 2000. The middle 50 percent earned less than $21,050, and the highest 10 percent earned more than $87,770. According to the Society of Stage Directors and Choreographers, summer theatres offer compensation, including royalties (based on the number of performances), usually ranging from $2,500 to $8,000 for a three- to four-week run of a production. Directing a production at a dinner theatre usually pays less than a summer theatre but has more potential for royalties. Regional theatres may hire directors for longer periods of time, increasing compensation accordingly. The highest-paid directors work on Broadway productions, typically earning $50,000 plus royalties.

Producers seldom earn a set fee. Instead, they get a percentage of a show's earnings or ticket sales.

Playwrights, dramaturgs, and puppeteers earn wildly fluctuating incomes depending upon how much work they can get. Their jobs are traditionally supplemented by separate full-time jobs.

The large number of people desiring acting careers and the lack of formal entry requirements should continue to cause keen competition for actor, director, and producer jobs. Employment in these areas is expected to grow faster than the average for all occupations through 2010. Although a growing number will aspire to enter these professions, many will leave the field early because the work, when available, is hard, the hours are long, and the pay is low. Only artists with the most stamina and talent will find steady employment.

Growth of opportunities in recorded media should be accompanied by increasing jobs in live productions. Increasing numbers of people who enjoy live theatrical entertainment will continue to attend theatre performances for excitement and aesthetics. Touring productions of Broadway plays and other large shows are providing new opportunities for actors and directors.

However, employment may be affected by government funding for the arts—a further decline in funding could dampen future employment growth in this segment of the entertainment industry. In these financially uncertain times, regular grant writing has become second nature to theatre artists. Workers leaving the field will continue to create more job openings than will growth.

In the winter, most employment opportunities on the stage are in New York and other large cities, many of which have established professional regional theatres. In the summer, stock companies in suburban and resort areas also provide employment. Cruise lines and amusement parks regularly hold auditions for performers as well.

In addition, many cities have small nonprofit professional companies, which feature local amateur talent and professional entertainers. Normally, casts are selected in New York City for shows that go on the road. To get an idea of the endless success of certain productions, review the history of the epic Cameron Mackintosh–produced musical, *Les Misérables*, by Alain Boublil, Claude-Michel Schönberg, and Herbert Kretzmer. Based on the Victor Hugo novel about the plight of one condemned man and his dogged pursuer, the operatic show opened in 1985 and finally stopped touring the globe in 2002 (with productions in Japanese, French, German, and other languages). It joins the ranks of other long-running musicals, like *The Fantastiks*, *A Chorus Line*, and *Cats*.

For More Information

Lincoln High School: Academic, Visual and Performing Arts
Magnet
555 Dana Avenue
San Jose, CA 95126
www.lincolnhighsanjose.org

Actors Equity Association
165 West Forty-Sixth Street
New York, NY 10036
www.actorsequity.org

American Alliance for Theatre and Education (AATE)
Theatre Department
Arizona State University
Box 872002
Tempe, AZ 85287
www.aate.com

American Federation of Television and Radio Artists (AFTRA)
260 Madison Avenue, Seventh Floor
New York, NY 10016
www.aftra.org

Center for Puppetry Arts
1404 Spring Street NW
Atlanta, GA 30309
www.puppet.org

Emerson College
Performing Arts Department
120 Boylston Street
Boston, MA 02116
www.emerson.edu

Ithaca College
Theatre Arts Program
School of Humanities and Sciences
201 Muller Center
Ithaca, NY 14850
www.ithaca.edu

National Association of Schools of Theater
11250 Roger Bacon Drive, Suite 21
Reston, VA 20190
www.arts-accredit.org

Screen Actors Guild (SAG)
5757 Wilshire Boulevard
Los Angeles, CA 90036
www.sag.org

Theatre Communications Group
520 Eighth Avenue, Twenty-Fourth Floor
New York, NY 10018
www.tcg.org

Union-Internationale de la Marionnette (UNIMA)
10, Cours Aristide Brand
B.P. 402
08107 Charleville-Mézières
France
www.unima.org

UNIMA-USA
1404 Spring Street NW
Atlanta, GA 30309
www.unima-usa.org

CHAPTER THREE

Careers in Dance

Although it's more than fifty years old, the British film *The Red Shoes* remains a timeless example of the relentless dedication required of professional dancers. Revolving around a young, driven ballerina named Victoria Paige, played by Moira Shearer of London's former Sadler's Wells Ballet, it addresses—albeit somewhat melodramatically—the intense sacrifices and critical choices faced by artists in a profession that can take a daunting toll on one's body and emotional state.

When the Svengaliesque ballet director asks Victoria, "Why does one dance?" she prophetically counters with another question, "Why does one live?" That belief still rings true today as dancers essentially live their careers. Their bodies are their instruments. Besides stretching their bodies into aesthetically beautiful but completely unnatural positions, they have to lead healthy lifestyles and continually monitor their calorie intake.

Daily classes are a given, as well as long rehearsals and extensive performance bookings. Whether you choose classical ballet, modern, tap, ethnic, jazz, or ballroom, be prepared to put in intense hours of training on a daily basis.

Dance is a field where choreographers, artistic directors, and teachers all studied dance and/or performed in a professional capacity. There is an incredible amount of overlap, and often the lines blur across these specializations. Travel is also an integral part of the dance profession at large.

The regional dance movement has spawned great successes outside New York City, long regarded as the epicenter of dance. That is not to say that Manhattan's dance life has dwindled. It is still bustling with eclectic movement and new, experimental choreography. And the exciting part is that other cities have caught the wave. Cities with full-time professional dance companies include Atlanta, Boston, Chicago, Cincinnati, Cleveland, Columbus, Dallas, Houston, Miami, Milwaukee, Philadelphia, Pittsburgh, Salt Lake City, San Francisco, Seattle, and Washington, D.C. Companies in Canada include Alberta Ballet, Ballet British Columbia, and Royal Winnipeg Ballet.

A substantial contingent of American dancers have settled into companies in Europe, attracted by a more generous attitude toward the arts and an attentiveness to the dancers' quality of life through competitive salaries, insurance benefits, and reasonable housing.

Dancer exchange programs give performers from other countries an opportunity to study in the United States, and vice versa. These programs also help broaden a dancer's experiences and ranges of interpretation.

Dancers

Because dance involves so many subcategories, it is difficult to lump all dancers together. Classical ballet, one of the most demanding of the performing arts, fosters a different approach or method than the modern or tap wizards. And, due to the varying degrees of muscle stress and endurance involved, the categories demand different retirement ages. In general, all dancers should have a solid foundation of ballet training in order to move gracefully from one medium to the next.

When it comes to classical ballet, age is a major issue. Girls begin training as young as three years old, while boys often start much later (twelve years old or early teens). Because pointe, or toe, work is required of girls, they must build strength in their feet, legs, and spine. Boys concentrate more on grand, or bravura, movements such as high jumps and turns.

Major classical ballet companies are affiliated with a school from which many dancers are chosen to serve as apprentices. A career-growth path begins in the corps de ballet, or ensemble, then proceeds to soloist level before attaining principal dancer ranks. For men, the highest rank is premiere danseur; for women, prima ballerina *assoluta.*

Dancers' careers will most likely carry them through the ranks of a large-scale ballet company, where they would probably peak in their twenties and early thirties, before thinking of retirement at forty. Of course, the late Margot Fonteyn was still dancing *Romeo and Juliet* in her sixties, and Rudolf Nureyev danced until his death in 1993 at age fifty-four. However, they are most definitely the exceptions, not the rules.

Many classical dancers take the teaching or choreographic route after retiring from the stage. Another option is being named artistic director of a company. Others, like Mikhail Baryshnikov, extend their performing lives by joining modern dance companies, which do not require the extreme strain and rigidity of pointe work (for women). Baryshnikov went on to lead the experimental White Oak Dance Project, which tours the world. Modern dancers are more interested in exploring new ways of moving and using the entire body as a form of deeply personal or highly sociopolitical expression.

The modern tap renaissance—launched in the 1980s with Broadway hits like *Black and Blue* and *Bring in 'da Funk, Bring in 'da Noise,* starring mega-tapper Savion Glover—continues to expand. Dancer-choreographer Lane Alexander heads the Chicago Human Rhythm Project (CHRP), one of the largest tap and rhythmic dance festivals in the country. Established in 1991, the annual August festival includes master classes featuring guest artists and a gala performance. Most recently, CHRP has been showcasing international rhythmic artists and instituted an annual youth tap conference. Tap festivals are also held in other major cities, such as New York, San Francisco, and St. Louis. Tap involves complex rhythmic, percussive exercises, and its devotees range in age from two to one hundred.

Jazz, tap, modern, ballet, and ethnic dancing all tie into routines choreographed for musical theatre performers. Ballroom dancing may also be required, but that's an area reserved more for Olympic-modeled competitions than for entertainment.

Staying healthy and at a reasonable weight should be part of a dancer's daily routine. Stories of eating disorders, drug use, and excessive smoking are frequently reported within this pressure-filled, highly body-conscious profession.

Young women seem most susceptible to anexoria and bulimia in an effort to stay as slim as they perceive their competition to be. It's well established that anorexic dancers are not healthy. Their condition can lead to permanent internal damage and even death. If you are prone to such disorders, seek counseling immediately. A healthy weight can be maintained by eating right, getting enough rest, and exercising properly. Health also has a lot to do with attitude and self-perception. Never let anyone in the dance profession lead you to believe that your success or failure is determined by your weight.

Now that we've entered the twenty-first century, the adaptable, well-rounded, healthy dancer will be in the greatest demand as multiple forms of dance begin to merge and appeal to culturally, socially, and economically diverse audiences.

Getting Started

The most significant first move in pursuing a dance career is finding the right school. It's okay for parents to enroll their tots in some type of movement class at the local park district to familiarize them with structured physical activity. But if a child expresses a burning desire to dance, and has the talent to match, a program run by seasoned, professional, patient, caring, trustworthy, well-connected experts will truly get a young dancer's career off to a soaring start.

Related classes, such as music, acting, and art, also enhance a dancer's approach to this ethereal profession. A solid foundation allows performers to branch out in many directions. And, we can't forget the obvious: properly fitted shoes, sold by dance sales representatives, not only make well-executed movement possible but also help bones develop properly.

Since a great part of the dancer's energy comes from within, supplementing rigorous classes with yoga sessions or daily meditation tunes the mind for the demands, disappointments, and pressures of the field.

Performing experience is essential for gaining a certain level of comfort and confidence on stage. School variety shows and dance recitals teach young performers how it all comes together. There is also a rise in semiprofessional youth dance companies affiliated with dance schools. Learning famous variations, such as *Swan Lake, Act II*, Martha Graham's *Letter to the World*, and classic tap combinations will prepare you for the big time.

It is also wise to audition for summer dance camps and weekend workshops or conventions held throughout the year. Most offer scholarships and afford students the chance to study with renowned guest artists and work with dancers from a variety of backgrounds and schools.

Choreographers, Artistic Directors, Managing Directors, and Ballet Masters

Choreographers are in essence playwrights who use movement instead of words to tell a story or convey a feeling. In short, they create original dances. Coming from dance backgrounds gives them the advantage of knowing how dancers move and what kinds of combinations can be aesthetically executed.

Freelance choreographers are commissioned to develop dances for a troupe. Some work in residence with an established dance company. Frequently, the artistic director also serves as a choreographer for the company he or she heads.

Being an artistic director requires excellent organizational, communication, and management skills. Artistic directors work closely with a company's board of directors on programming choices, fund-raising efforts, and outreach projects. Often, they direct a company's affiliated school. Additionally, artistic directors are expected to audition, hire, and fire dancers; lead rehearsals; and attend all the performances. It is a high-pressure job with many intangible rewards.

The managing director's role is similar to the producer's: keeping an eye on the finances. The managing director works with the board of directors to organize fund-raisers, subscription drives, and other creative venues to keep the company in the black. Together with the artistic director, the managing director also writes grant proposals to help offset production costs of new works.

For professional dancers well versed in a company's repertoire, moving on to become ballet masters is a respectable and enduring way of passing on one's knowledge. They teach company classes, are involved in the rehearsal process, and work one-on-one with lead dancers. They also set established dances on companies. These gifted individuals are in residence with dance companies around the world.

Getting Started

Choreographers and their colleagues—with the exception of managing directors—typically get started the same way dancers do. They differ, however, in the area of artistic creativity and leadership. You may be a stunning dancer but have absolutely no talent or desire for creating dances or directing a company. Choreographers can get their starts by staging the dance sections of their high school musicals or dance school annual recitals. Many enter choreographic competitions, where company artistic directors may be scouting for new ideas and talent. Some simply start their own companies.

When it comes to making your mark with major dance troupes, though, you mainly have to rise through the ranks and put in your time as a dancer and as a dance insider. Artistic directors display personalities conducive to managing an array of temperamental artists and generate forward-looking ideas that will advance the art form and keep a company fresh. They are also sensitive to their audiences' needs and to the kinds of works that are realistically marketable.

Managing directors, who come from financial or arts management backgrounds, make sure the artistic director doesn't get too carried away with his or her creativity. They bring with them a savvy blend of numeric know-how and a deep understanding of the inner workings of the dance administrative structure.

Ballet masters begin by coaching small groups of dancers. Many even study "labanotation," a complex method of recording on paper entire ballets and dances. They also immerse themselves in the history of a particular work in order to pass the nuances of style, mood, and period accuracies of the piece on to their students.

Educational and Apprenticeship Requirements for Dance Professionals

Training and practice never end for dance professionals. They take classes every day and spend many additional hours perfecting their skills and rehearsing. Their teachers become their mentors, their role models, and often their greatest inspirations. Because of the strenuous and time-consuming training required, a dancer's formal academic instruction may be minimal. However, a general education in music, literature, history, and the visual arts is helpful in the interpretation of dramatic episodes, ideas, and feelings.

Many colleges and universities confer bachelor's or higher degrees in dance, usually through the departments of physical education, music, theatre, or fine arts. Most programs concentrate on modern dance but also offer courses in ballet and classical techniques, dance composition, dance history, dance criticism, and movement analysis.

A college education is not essential to obtain employment as a professional dancer. In fact, ballet dancers who postpone their first audition until graduation may compete at a disadvantage with younger dancers. On the other hand, a college degree can help the dancer who retires at an early age (which happens often) and wishes to enter another field of work.

Completion of a college program in dance and education is essential to qualify for employment as a college, elementary, or high school dance teacher. Colleges, as well as conservatories, generally require graduate degrees, but performance experience often may be substituted. A college background is not necessary for teaching dance or choreographing professionally. Studio schools usually require teachers to have experience as performers.

The dancer's life is one of rigorous practice and self-discipline. Therefore, patience, perseverance, and a devotion to the art form are essential. Good health and physical stamina are necessary in order to follow a rugged schedule of classes, rehearsals, and performances. Above all, you must have flexibility, agility, coordination, grace, musicality, a sense of rhythm, and a creative ability to express yourself through movement.

Dancers seldom perform unaccompanied, so they must be able to function as part of an ensemble. They should be highly motivated and condition themselves to face the anxiety of intermittent employment and rejections when auditioning for work.

The Art of Auditioning

Auditioning is essential to a dancer's career path. Industry magazines, such as *Dance Magazine*, *Dance Teacher*, and *Dance Spirit*, publish audition notices for all types of dance environments—classical ballet, modern, jazz, tap, and Broadway musicals. They also post auditions on their corresponding websites, and dancers can always browse the Internet for online audition notices. One of the best ways to prepare for an audition is to participate in dance competitions like the USA International Ballet Competition and the Grand Prix. On a smaller scale, most dancers enroll in summer intensive workshops taught by well-respected faculty and have a chance to audition for performances at the end of the session.

The most effective auditioning advice is focused on artists' emotional states more than their technical prowess. Some of the best advice, based on conversations with various dancers over the years, includes: focus and concentrate on your strongest qualities; avoid the temptation to compare yourself to your fellow competitors; be yourself; and have fun. For dancers pursuing Broadway dance work, keep in mind that, as part of a musical ensemble, you will most likely be required to sing and even read dialogue in addition to being able to dance a range of eclectic choreography. Former Broadway dance star Ann Reinking heads the Broadway Theatre Project, a series of master classes taught every summer in Tampa, Florida, and geared toward preparing young dancers for musical-theatre dance careers.

In the August 1996 issue of *Dance Magazine*, Linda Hamilton wrote an in-depth feature on the joys and perils of auditioning. She interviewed a group of dancers who auditioned in downtown Manhattan for Twyla Tharp's touring company. About eight hundred dancers showed up for only twelve available positions. The odds were against most of them.

According to Hamilton: "One dancer who decided to audition anyway was Claudia Zairos, a twenty-six-year-old professional from Long Island. Her strategy at auditions is to pretend that she is performing onstage rather than trying to convince herself and others that she is right for the position. She says, 'Some people say it helps if you think you're great and you're gonna get the part. But then, if you do end up being rejected, it hurts more because it reflects on your dancing.' To get up her nerve before a tryout, Zairos listens to friends who 'tell me that I really come out when I perform.'"

"The other dancers who were interviewed also used a constructive approach to the audition process by regarding it as a valuable dance experience, a free class, or a chance to work with a famous choreographer," adds the writer.

Another contender, Dawn Ann Bryant, takes the constructive approach of not paying attention to the competition. When she forgets to focus on her creative strengths, her negative thoughts come down to body type: "You look at people who are taller, who have longer legs, longer extensions," she says. "You start to think, 'My legs aren't that long. My extension isn't that high.'"

"Dawn is aware that this kind of thinking is destructive," Hamilton adds. "Instead, keep your attention on what you can do."

A Profile of a Dance Program

Following is Lucia Mauro's story detailing Northwestern University's dance program, which appeared in *Dance Teacher* magazine.

"Turning out performers is not our only goal," states Susan A. Lee, Ph.D., director of Northwestern University's dance program. "We're preparing them for lifetime involvement in the field. For me, part of what our students are doing is trying on a life."

The program, which is a branch of the Theatre Department at the Evanston, Illinois, liberal arts university, achieves this well-rounded mission by integrating academic and performance aspects of dance. Students create a program by selecting courses from three core areas: performance/choreography; history/theory/criticism; and professional studies, which includes labanotation, dance in education, dance and expressive arts therapies, and dance science. Studies are rooted in modern and jazz and supported with ballet. Other forms—ethnic, tap, and hip-hop—are offered.

"We definitely have [current and past] students all over the map," adds Lee, "and that's exactly what we want."

Alumni have gone on to careers in arts administration, dance therapy (like Pilates and Feldenkreis), dance education, Broadway musicals, and mixed media (incorporating dance and video). Others are independent choreographers or have started their own companies.

Grace Applefeld, who graduated in 2002 with a B.S. in dance and a second major in creative writing, recently was hired as assistant to the marketing director at the Joffrey Ballet of Chicago.

"Northwestern lets you explore other options," says Applefeld, "and I was able to balance academics with practical experience. I took modern dance technique, and I took classes in dance education and administration—even Dance in Hollywood Movie Musicals. They encourage you to be involved with all different parts of dance. It's not just about performance; it's also about managing a company, teaching, and art therapy."

Applefeld, who interned at the Kennedy Center in Washington, D.C., plans to pursue a career in arts administration but also foresees possibilities in arts writing and dance criticism.

In its commitment to showing students a wide spectrum of dance opportunities, Northwestern does not downplay movement and choreography. It mainly places equal value on those eclectic areas.

"We support and nurture other fields," says Lee," to allow students to find their personal expressive identity, as well as embrace other diverse voices.

"In a larger sense, we've created an environment to help them know where they're headed—and to acknowledge that the body can be a fragile thing. Careers are unpredictable. We want our students to be prepared. We don't ever want them to have to give up their dreams."

Northwestern University, a well-respected research institution with an outstanding Theatre Department (based within the School of Speech), has a significant reputation in the arts. Dance majors study in-depth choreographic process and craft. They are also required to write, research, and analyze and continue to develop technically. Full-time dance program faculty—currently numbering eleven—are active professional choreographers, performers, researchers, and scholars. They include Billy Siegenfeld of Jump Rhythm Jazz Project; scholar Susan Manning; and Erin Harper, a Pilates expert. Guest artists complement their work.

"We look for faculty with an all-encompassing sensibility," notes Lee. "We're asking them to take all those life experiences and create art. They are constantly thinking and doing and articulating in order to reach higher levels of understanding."

The brain and body are equally exercised. And performance opportunities are plentiful. The Northwestern University Dance Ensemble (N.U.D.E.) presents student choreography and performance. DanceWorks features choreography by faculty and guest artists. Students also may produce their own concerts in conjunction with course work or independent projects. The Music Theatre Program provides additional opportunities to develop work and be on stage.

Jenny Shore, a senior dance major, is artistic director of the jazz-based Graffiti Dancers, a student-run company in existence at Northwestern since the inception of the dance program in 1979. The troupe incorporates other disciplines, like ballet and modern.

"I've been able to discover that choreographing is more artistically satisfying than performing," says Shore. "I actually didn't start out as a dance major. I got exposed to the program through a DanceWorks [faculty] performance. I was attracted to its noncompetitive nature and how it embraced people's different styles and interests."

Shore has tacked on a communication major—a common move by most Northwestern University students, whose interests may not be restricted to one area. In fact, Lee reports that there are twenty declared undergraduate dance majors, but hundreds of students are involved in the program. They might be premed students who want to learn more about anatomy or plan to pursue performing arts medicine (a field Lee sees as a big growth area), or electrical engineers who specialize in designing dance-related websites.

Cross-disciplinary studies have been encouraged at the university in general. And Joseph Mills, a full-time dance faculty member, is one of its greatest champions. A former dancer with Erick Hawkins Dance and Momix, he teaches modern technique, anatomy and kinesiology, and movement analysis. He's also planning to collaborate with a music professor on an inter-arts course.

"The health of the dance program can be attributed to its place in one of the nation's top theatre programs," explains Mills. "At Northwestern, the potential for collaboration and interdisciplinary work is very strong."

Most recently, Mills helped develop a movement-theatre piece, *Drums on the Dam* (based on the first English translation of a French play), as a workshop production. He joined together dance and theatre students "to explore a variety of approaches to the text," including mask work.

When it comes to his modern technique classes, Mills's goal is for dancers to be "intellectually engaged in movement rather than merely executing steps."

"If you concentrate only on technique," he continues, "you may be technically sound, but the movement has no soul or thought behind it."

He favors Erick Hawkins' philosophical approach, which involves breathing life into movement—experiencing the weight of the body on a count rather than focusing only on being on the right count. "I challenge students to think of the movement and where it comes from," says Mills. "Hawkins valued a noninjurious technique and the dancers' experience of the movement. I'm trying to inculcate an embodied form of movement rather than the outer shell of movement shapes."

Since he performed with Momix, Mills also injects a playfulness and athleticism into his classes.

The faculty reflects Lee's holistic dance-education theory. Lee—who teaches composition and dance history, therapy, education, and criticism—studied modern dance and, over the years, discovered her love of teaching. As a dance teacher at the high school level, she became acutely aware of the anxieties of young students—an issue she felt was rarely addressed in dance programs.

She then went back to school to receive a Ph.D. in psychology from Northwestern University's School of Education. In 1979, Lee was invited to start a dance program at Northwestern. At the time, she recalls, dance had been a small part of the physical education department. Yet, she notes, there was a divide between the arts and science arenas. "These folks weren't talking to each other," Lee says, "and that bothered me."

An official dance program was begun through the Theatre Department, and Lee immediately stressed a holistic philosophy. She attributes its growth to the high caliber of the faculty and students. Both groups are equally committed to developing as educators and as artists.

A key area of focus has been maintaining an open and collaborative dialogue among the faculty. Lee enthuses, "There's something very magical about these folks. We don't experience the kind of rivalry one might experience in another setting. We continually examine how do you continue to set high standards and challenge faculty and students without tipping into an unhealthy competitive realm."

One way is by fostering an ongoing teach-and-learn model. Faculty mentor students yet give majors the opportunity to contribute to the creation of dance performance. Both groups teach dance on the middle school and high school levels through Northwestern's outreach programs. So those nurturing relationships are part of the school's natural fiber. Lee stresses, "It's important that students see the faculty as artists and teachers; that they see the belief system that informs what they do in the classroom."

The director cites two pivotal moments in the dance program's growth. The first was getting the undergraduate B.S. dance major launched in 1997 through Northwestern's School of Speech. Previously, students enrolled in a certificate program or minored in dance. On the graduate level, students can do a concentration in dance for an M.A. and receive a Ph.D. in theatre and drama.

The second was acquiring a facility for classes and performances in 1982. Producer Gary Marshall, a Northwestern University alum, funded the dance program's Marjorie Ward Marshall Dance Center to honor his mother, who was a dancer.

This state-of-the-art building, which faces the lakefront, consists of offices, two large studios, a rehearsal room that doubles as a tap classroom, and a more informal loft that serves as a classroom and as an experimental performance space. The Marjorie Ward Marshall Dance Center is part of the Theatre and Interpretation Center, which houses the Department of Theatre and the Department of Performance Studies. The dance program produces concerts at the adjoining proscenium-style 375-seat Josephine Louis Theatre and the nearby 1,000-seat Cahn Auditorium.

Lee reiterates Northwestern's stimulating mind-body theory: "I'm a firm believer in the idea that a university should happen to students," she says. "They should not just be getting through a program. The university should shake them up and challenge their belief systems. They should come out with a new sense of wondering and endless possibilities."

Where Are the Jobs?

Professional dancers work in a variety of settings, notably dance companies, theatres, dinner theatres, dance studios, restaurants, amusement parks, and cruise lines. In addition, there are many dance instructors in secondary schools, colleges, universities, and private studios. Many teachers also perform from time to time.

A marked change is that New York no longer has a monopoly on the plum dance jobs, even though it is still home to American Ballet Theatre, New York City Ballet, many modern companies, and the Broadway musical. Dance opportunities exist around the world. It's up to you to decide, then go for, whatever realm of dance gives you the greatest satisfaction.

Salary and Success Outlook for Dance Professionals

Professional dancers and choreographers held about twenty-six thousand jobs in 2000. Earnings are governed by union contracts. Dancers in the major opera ballet, classical ballet, and modern dance corps belong to the American Guild of Musical Artists Inc., AFL-CIO; those on live or videotaped television belong to the American Federation of Television and Radio Artists; those who perform in films and on television belong to the Screen Actors Guild; and those in musical theatre are members of the Actors Equity Association.

The unions and producers sign basic agreements specifying minimum salary rates, hours of work, benefits, and other conditions of employment. However, the contract each dancer signs with the producer of the show may be more favorable than the basic agreement.

Median annual earnings of dancers were $22,470 in 2000. The middle 50 percent earned between $14,260 and $34,600. The lowest 10 percent earned less than $12,520, and the highest 10 percent earned more than $55,220. Dancers on tour received an additional allowance for room and board.

Median annual earnings of choreographers were $27,010 in 2000. The middle 50 percent earned between $17,970 and $42,080. The lowest 10 percent earned less than $13,370, and the highest 10 percent earned more than $55,800. Median annual earnings were $25,860 in dance studios, schools, and halls.

Dancers' salaries are generally low because employment is irregular. They often must supplement their incomes by taking temporary jobs unrelated to dancing. Dancers covered by union contracts are entitled to some paid sick leave, paid vacations, and various health and pension benefits (including extended sick pay and childbirth provisions) provided by their unions. Employers contribute toward these benefits. Unfortunately, those not covered by union contracts do not enjoy such benefits.

Dancers and choreographers face very keen competition for jobs. The number of applicants will continue to exceed the number of job openings, and only the most talented will find regular work.

Employment of dance professionals is expected to increase about as fast as the average for all occupations through 2010 due to the public's continued interest in this form of artistic expression. However, government cuts in funding for the National Endowment for the Arts and related organizations could adversely affect employment in this field.

Although jobs will arise each year due to increased demand, most openings will happen as dancers and choreographers retire or leave the occupation for other reasons—and as dance companies continue to search for, and discover, outstanding talent.

The best job opportunities are expected to be with national dance companies because of the demand for performances outside New York City. Opera and theatre companies, television, movies, and dance groups affiliated with colleges and universities will offer increased employment opportunities (especially for dance teachers). Other growth areas include ballroom and spiritual dance (encompassing praise dance and related liturgical forms whose aim is to enhance worship services in various denominations).

With innovations such as electronic sounds and music videos, choreography is becoming a more challenging field of endeavor and will present more options for highly talented and creative individuals. Now Web surfers can download dance CD-ROMs on their computer screens. A whole new area of "computer choreography" and marketing strategy is breaking new ground for dancers and other performing artists.

· ·

For More Information

American Alliance for Health, Physical Education,
    Recreation and Dance
1900 Association Drive
Reston, VA 20191
www.aahperd.org

American Dance Guild
P.O. Box 2006
Lenox Hill Station
New York, NY 10021
www.americandanceguild.org

Dance/USA
1156 Fifteenth Street NW, Suite 820
Washington, DC 20005
www.danceusa.org

National Association of Schools of Dance
11250 Roger Bacon Drive, Suite 21
Reston, VA 20190
www.arts-accredit.org

Society of Stage Directors and Choreographers
1501 Broadway, Suite 1701
New York, NY 10036
www.ssdc.org

Broadway Theatre Project
USF 30539
University of South Florida
4202 East Fowler Avenue
Tampa, FL 33620
www.broadwaytp.org

Some High School Dance Programs

Chicago Academy for the Arts
1010 West Chicago Avenue
Chicago, IL 60622
www.chicagoacademyforthearts.org

Chicago Academy offers a private college preparatory program that combines academic study in theatre, dance, music, art, and creative writing. Admission is based on scholastic examinations and an audition. Classes include ballet, modern dance, jazz, pointe, pas de deux, composition, dance history, and kinesiology.

Fiorello H. LaGuardia High School of Music and Art and
    Performing Arts
100 Amsterdam Avenue
New York, NY 10023
www.laguardiahs.org

Founded in 1936—and immortalized in the movie Fame—*this renowned performing arts high school has earned an international reputation for excellence in the arts—from drama, dance, and music to theatrical design and visual art. Classes are taught by working professionals, and the program offers ample performing opportunities. Alumni include actress Jennifer Aniston and Academy Award–winning actor Adrien Brody, dancers Arthur Mitchell and Edward Vilella, and opera star Catherine Malfitano.*

Idyllwild Arts Academy
P.O. Box 38
Idyllwild, CA 92549
www.idyllwildarts.org

> *Students study ballet (including pas de deux, character, pointe, and men's classes), modern dance, jazz, and choreography. Students are accepted by audition.*

Los Angeles County High School for the Arts
5151 State University Drive
Library North 1034
Los Angeles, CA 90032
www.lafn.org

> *Located on the campus of California State University, the public high school focuses on modern dance, classical ballet, theatre, and visual art. It is tuition-free and combines regular academics with afternoon performance and dance studies.*

Orange County High School for the Arts
3591 Cerritos Avenue
Los Alamitos, CA 90720
www.ocsarts.net

> *The program has two primary facets: classical, traditional ballet and modern dance; and commercial dance that is oriented toward stage and show business. Courses in African dance, flamenco, and jazz dance are also included. The program is tuition-free.*

Educational Center for the Arts (ECA)
55 Audubon Street
New Haven, CT 06511

> *ECA offers afternoon training for students from school districts in the New Haven area. The curriculum provides training in technical and creative skills and develops an understanding of the many cultural and historical influences on the arts and how dance relates to other art forms.*

CHAPTER FOUR

Adventures in Music

"If music be the food of love, play on—give me excess of it!" implores the lovesick Duke Orsino in the opening lines of Shakespeare's *Twelfth Night*. Throughout history, humanity has beckoned music to describe what words cannot. It is transcendent, poetic, universal. According to Greek mythology, Zeus presented his son Apollo with a lute, which he played sweetly for his three Muses: Calliope (lyric poetry), Polyhymnia (mime), and Terpsichore (dance and song).

Music continues to engage us—whether we are at a concert, on hold, in an elevator, in our cars, or just about anywhere (thanks to headsets and high-powered cell phones). Today, the music industry is incomprehensibly vast and diverse. Classical musicians are about as far removed from grunge bands as ballerinas are from sumo wrestlers.

Actually, an entire book could be written on the music business alone. Styles of music include classical, opera, rock, pop, jazz, reggae, folk, rap, country western, ska, and ethnic. Nevertheless, this chapter aims to present a comprehensive overview of the field at large, with special attention given to musicians, singers, composers, lyricists, conductors, concertmasters, and choral directors.

Musicians held about 240,000 jobs in 2000. More than 40 percent worked part-time; more than 40 percent were self-employed. Touring is a major part of the business.

Musicians and singers are considered vital partners in the business, and, together with composers, they create some dynamic sounds. Conductors and concertmasters work primarily in the classical music field, leading their orchestras through the proper tempo and pace of symphonic music. There are also musical the-atre conductors as well as band directors (in schools and in the armed forces), whose repertoire runs the gamut from marches and patriotic songs to pop music.

Musicians

Overlap often exists in the music arena, where musicians play instruments, sing, compose, arrange, or conduct groups in instru-mental or vocal performances. Numerous performing venues are available to them. They may perform alone or as part of a group, before live audiences, on radio and television, or in recording stu-dios and movie productions.

It is common for musicians to specialize in a particular style as a way of defining themselves. They could go solo or play in an orchestra, band, rock group, or jazz ensemble. Instruments range from strings, brass, woodwinds, and percussion to electronic syn-thesizers and other digitally based systems. To improve employ-ment opportunities, some musicians master more than one instrument or combine expertise in, for example, piano and vio-lin for a fuller understanding of how instruments work together.

Young people who are considering careers in music should have musical talent, versatility, creative ability, poise, stage presence, and the ability to face large audiences. Since mastery of an instru-ment requires constant study and practice, self-discipline is vital. Musicians who play concert and nightclub engagements must have physical stamina for frequent night travel and late perfor-mances. They must also be prepared to face the anxiety of inter-mittent employment and rejections when auditioning for work.

Advancement for musicians generally means becoming better known by performing with renowned bands or orchestras. Suc-cessful musicians often rely on agents or managers to book per-forming engagements, negotiate contracts, and basically plan the course of their careers.

Singers

Singing is a natural outgrowth of playing; the voice can be another instrument in a band or an orchestra. While we have devoted a chapter to opera and have mentioned vocalists on the theatre pages, singers in general are grouped in the music category. Unless they only sing a cappella (that is, using no musical accompaniment), vocal artists unaccompanied would give only half-realized performances. Their aim is to interpret the melodies of music and harmonize with instruments in order for the entire aural experience to be complete.

Creating a style is paramount to establishing a loyal following. And age is irrelevant. Look at Tony Bennett, whose mass appeal has skyrocketed over the past decade. He recently collaborated with Canadian vocalist k.d. lang, whose vocal style runs the gamut of pop, rock, country-western, cabaret, and jazz.

Singers are traditionally classified according to their vocal range—soprano, contralto, tenor, baritone, or bass. Like musicians, they have endless outlets: theatres, stadiums, amusement parks, nightclubs, restaurants, cruise ships, television shows, commercials, and movies.

Composers and Lyricists

Just when you thought every possible song had been written, the airwaves are showered with totally new sounds, musical styles, and, yes, songs. We owe it all to composers and lyricists. Composers create original music, such as symphonies, operas, sonatas, or popular tunes. They transcribe ideas into musical notation using harmony, rhythm, melody, and tonal structure.

Most songwriters now compose and edit music using computers. They even have a musical keyboard linked to a computer, which compiles the digital information into musical notation while they play. And they can program the composition in musical notation into the computer, which in turn can play back the piece.

Composers can also work as arrangers, transcribing and adapting musical compositions to a specific style for orchestras, bands, choral groups, or individuals. Lyricists work key-to-key with composers and literally put words to music.

Conductors and Concertmasters

What may look like frenetic hand motions and head bobbing is really a conductor's complex, universal musical sign language that enables musicians to give an effective rendering of a composition. A conductor, who works together with a concertmaster for repertoire selection and in rehearsals, must have a deep understanding of every instrument in an orchestra.

Conductors, or baton virtuosi, must be sensitive to subtle changes in tonal quality, timbre, and tempo and must have a thorough knowledge of the composers whose masterpieces they bring to life again and again.

They are responsible for auditioning and selecting musicians, choosing the musical programs, and directing rehearsals and performances. They apply intricate conducting techniques to achieve desired musical effects.

Choral Directors

Choral directors lead choirs and glee clubs, sometimes working with band or orchestra conductors. They also audition and select singers and lead rehearsals. During performances, they conduct, aiming to achieve harmony, rhythm, tempo, shading, and other substantial musical effects.

Choral competitions exist around the world—especially in England, where they began centuries ago. Children's choruses also have been springing up across the country. Contrary to their ecclesiastical origins, choral performances are not restricted to places of worship. They have successfully spilled over into the secular realm.

"And a 1-2-3, Hit It!"—Getting Your Career Off the Ground

Getting off to a good start in the music industry can happen at any age, depending on which segment of the business you wish to pursue. The late pianist-satirist Victor Borge—who began studying as a child—continued to attract crowds to his musical-parody concerts into the 1990s. Ageless cellist Yo-Yo Ma keeps finding innovative and educational ways to promote classical music from around the world, including teaming up with other celebrities and instituting the Silk Road concert tour.

Rock stars, for the most part, are naturally among the younger generation. However, Mick Jagger, Keith Richards, and their acid-rock compadres continue to blaze the touring trail. There seems to be no end to Paul McCartney's reinventions of himself on stage. Now Lisa Marie Presley has followed in her legendary father's footsteps to break into the pop-rock biz in her thirties.

Mozart, of course, was a child prodigy whose work improved with age. Songwriter Randy Newman hit it big in pop music as a young man, then went on to write scores for musicals, such as *Faust*. Britney Spears, Jewel, and Pink represent an ongoing female pop-culture lineage. All the Marsalis brothers have made great strides in jazz and classical music under the guidance of their famous father, Ellis Marsalis.

These examples also show how fragmented yet interconnected the music industry is. Career paths can tend to bounce all over the map.

Music permeates our society, so limitless venues exist to test its sonorous waters. School shows and community theatre productions are common starting points, but recitals and musical competitions can be experienced at a much younger age. Clubs and restaurants, as well as gigs at bars, neighborhood festivals, and special occasions, have given many musical artists their first breaks.

As in all the performing arts, begin with an outstanding teacher or mentor who takes a serious interest in your abilities. For a touching, realistic glimpse into the joys of teaching and learning music, rent the film *Mr. Holland's Opus,* in which Richard Dreyfuss gives a tour de force performance as a longtime high school music teacher who instills confidence, a sense of accomplishment, and crucial life lessons in all of his students.

Educational and Apprenticeship Requirements

Although age is not as serious a concern in music as it is in dance, many music professionals begin studying voice or an instrument at an early age. They gain vital performing experience by playing in a school or community band or orchestra or with a group of friends. Singers usually start training when their voices mature. No doubt, there are legends—such as Ethel Merman and Engelbert Humperdinck—who never had a voice lesson in their lives. But remember, they are rare examples of natural megatalent.

Participation in school musicals or in a choir provides solid early training and experience. Musicians need extensive and ongoing training in order to acquire the necessary skill, knowledge, and ability to interpret music. Methods of training involve private study with an accomplished musician; college, university, or conservatory music programs; or thorough practice with an ensemble.

An audition is commonly required for entry into a formal music program, such as New York's Juilliard School. Courses include musical theory, music interpretation, composition, conducting, and instrumental and voice instruction. Composers, conductors, concertmasters, arrangers, and choral directors need advanced training in these subjects as well.

Many colleges, universities, and music conservatories grant bachelor's or higher degrees in music. Many also grant degrees in music education to qualify graduates for a state certificate to teach music in an elementary or secondary school. Opportunities to study with music masters around the world are plentiful.

Those who perform popular music must have a feel and understanding for the style of music that interests them. But classical training is a firm foundation from which they can expand their employment opportunities, as well as their musical talents. As a rule, musical artists take lessons with private teachers when young and seize every opportunity to make amateur or professional appearances.

Let's look at a sample music education program. Indiana University in Bloomington ranks as one of the top classical music training centers in the country. It offers undergraduate and graduate degrees in music. Courses encompass the recording arts, brass, church music, percussion, music education and pedagogy, conducting, composition, music therapy, music history and literature, voice, strings, harp, guitar, piano, organ, woodwinds, and early music. There are numerous performance opportunities in a range of ensembles—from bands and orchestras to early music and university choral groups—as well as master classes and private lessons.

Finding a Job in the Music World

Many musical artists work in cities where entertainment and recording activities are concentrated, such as New York, Los Angeles, and Nashville. But outlets exist throughout the country. Classical musicians may perform with professional orchestras or in small chamber music groups such as quartets and trios. Or they may play for opera, ballet, or musical theatre productions.

Interestingly, a lot of organists play in churches and synagogues; in fact, two out of three musicians who are paid a salary work in religious organizations.

Opportunities are also abundant in clubs and restaurants and at special events (such as weddings or neighborhood festivals). Well-known musicians and groups give their own concerts, appear "live" on radio and television, make recordings and music videos, or go on concert tours. Even the armed forces offer careers in their bands and smaller musical groups.

Technology allows more pop-oriented bands to burn their own CDs right on their computers. And, while it's great to play at clubs for experience, a more popular strategy is for bands to hire the best players to help produce a highly professional CD that is then sent to potential agents, managers, and producers. Bands continue to play the college circuits and get air time on college radio stations. But, ultimately, rapid technological progress, information overload, and short attention spans are pushing these musicians into getting their music heard on radio and TV at greater speeds.

One of the biggest challenges facing musicians who want to start their own pop-rock or alternative band is fans' ability to download music for free on the Internet. Countless articles have been written about label managers wishing to sue fans who download music from file-sharing sites, such as Kazaa and Lime Wire. In the late 1990s and dawn of the new millennium, free music downloading gave smaller labels a chance to compete with bigger labels by creating a "buzz" around a band's music. However, it soon turned into a way for the public to get music for free—cutting into artists' profits.

On June 25, 2003, the Recording Industry Association of America declared it would sue file sharers who ignore copyright laws. Another less extreme solution currently appears to be Apple Computer's iTunes Music Store, which allows consumers to download music for a fee. Music and the Internet will undoubtedly keep provoking new laws and trends. Now that fans can customize their own CDs, based on the songs they download, artists may no longer have to think in terms of making albums that come out once a year. They may be more successful writing singles regularly and getting them on the airwaves and online. Other artists tour festival circuits around the world and sell their own CDs.

....

Salary and Success Outlook for Music Professionals

Earnings often depend on a performer's professional reputation and place of employment, as well as on the number of hours worked. The most successful musical artists can earn far more than the minimum salaries indicated below.

According to the American Federation of Musicians, minimum salaries in major orchestras ranged from $24,720 to $100,196 per year during the 2000–2001 performing season. Each orchestra works out a separate contract with its local union. The seasons of these top orchestras ranged from twenty-four to fifty-two weeks, with eighteen orchestras reporting fifty-two-week contracts.

In regional orchestras, minimum salaries are often less because fewer performances are scheduled. Community orchestras often have more limited levels of funding and offer salaries much lower for seasons of shorter duration. Regional orchestra musicians often are paid per service without guarantees.

Artists employed by some symphony orchestras work under master wage agreements, which guarantee a season's work up to fifty-two weeks. Many other musicians may face relatively long periods of unemployment between jobs. Even when employed, however, a high percentage work part-time. Therefore, their earnings generally are lower than those in many other occupations. Since they may not work steadily for one employer, some performers cannot qualify for unemployment compensation, and few have either sick leave or paid vacations. For these reasons, many musicians and their colleagues give private lessons or take jobs unrelated to music to supplement their earnings as performers.

Many musicians belong to a local of the American Federation of Musicians. Professional singers usually belong to a branch of the American Guild of Musical Artists.

Competition for music-related jobs is keen, and talent alone is no guarantee of success. Yet the glamour and potentially high earnings attract many talented individuals. Overall employment of musicians is expected to grow about as fast as the average for all occupations through 2010. Almost all new wage and salary jobs for musicians will arise in religious organizations, where the majority of these workers are employed. Average growth is also expected for self-employed musicians who perform in nightclubs, concert tours, and other venues. The current pattern indicates that most job openings for music professionals will arise from the need to replace those who leave the field each year because they are unable to make a living solely as musicians.

Median annual earnings of salaried musicians and singers were $36,740 in 2000. The middle 50 percent earned between $19,590 and $59,330. Median annual earnings were $41,520 in the producers, orchestras, and entertainment industry, and $16,570 in religious organizations. Median annual earnings of salaried music directors and composers were $31,510 in 2000. The middle 50 percent earned between $21,080 and $45,000.

Earnings often depend on the number of weeks worked as well as the performer's professional reputation. The performance setting also affects pay rates.

Advancement for professional musicians usually means becoming better known and, therefore, performing for higher earnings. Successful musicians often rely on agents or managers to find them performing engagements, negotiate contracts, and develop their careers.

Interviews with Music Professionals

The following articles by the author originally appeared in Pioneer Press newspapers. They provide insight into the fields of classical music and musical composition and are reprinted here with permission.

....

Harpist Elizabeth Cifani

Elizabeth Cifani, who has played the harp for terminally ill patients in hospitals, regards the instrument as a great source of comfort for most listeners.

"The harp has a transformational effect on people," reflects the musician, who resides in Evanston, Illinois. "There's a pure quality to the sound, like that of a flute.

"I've been asked to play the harp at very dramatic points in people's lives—weddings and funerals. In fact, the Egyptian harp was a funeral instrument played by priestesses."

This doesn't necessarily mean that its lovely strings sing mainly of death and bereavement. According to Cifani, who has performed as principal harpist for Chicago's Lyric Opera since 1968, the harp can be very uplifting, exciting, and relaxing.

Acknowledging that, until recent years, the harp remained fairly inaccessible to most people because of its expense and difficulty in mastering, Cifani has set out to make it a more attainable option for music students. As a professor of harp at Northwestern University in Evanston, Cifani gives highly personalized instruction to a handful of harp majors that goes beyond learning proper technique.

"I'm a great believer in one-on-one teaching and open discussions that address creating and finding work for harpists, training opportunities, and dealing with stress," says the musician.

Her natural sense of humor emerged in some of her comments about the instrument's unique challenges: "The harp is like a big barometer," Cifani snickers. "It's very sensitive to heat, humidity, drafts, and body heat. When I see the auditorium filling up, I know I have to do some serious retuning. Also, the strings are prone to breaking, and harpists must tune their own instruments. Tuning is monstrous and constant."

Escalating into laughter, Cifani cites Garrison Keilor's comparison of the harp to caring for an aging relative: "It won't compromise and can't get in and out of cars!"

She does not think harps are that close to pianos, because a harpist is actually touching the strings. A pianist has a large mechanism covering those strings, as well as black keys for sharps and flats. Cifani uses pedals to create those same "accidentals."

Known for her solo work, the accomplished artist also considers herself a soloist within an orchestra. After all, there really isn't a harp "section." During the Lyric Opera's mammoth production of Wagner's *The Ring Cycle*, Cifani was essentially her own music director: "I approach all notes as potential solos."

For Cifani, the decision to become a harpist was made practically at birth in her native New Orleans. Her mother played the harp and violin. So the harp was always there, and as a toddler, Cifani claims, "I couldn't keep my little paws off."

Until she left for higher musical studies at Northwestern University, the musician was instructed by her mother. Nevertheless, Cifani has not lost her childlike fearlessness.

"Many musicians forget to operate 'in child mode,'" she comments. "They must lose themselves entirely in their work. When I'm performing, I think in music, not words."

Composer Mark Camphouse

From an ideological and historic standpoint, Rosa Parks, General Douglas MacArthur, Jack London, and Helen Keller couldn't be farther apart. Together, they would create quite a ruckus at a dinner party. Yet composer Mark Camphouse has made them the subjects of his socially conscious musical works. The fact that these were "great people with great minds who made a huge impact on American life and society" links them musically in the prolific writer's mind.

Tackling another prevalent topic, the "national epidemic of child abuse," Camphouse wrote "Watchman, Tell Us of the Night."

"It's vitally important that all those involved in the arts—educators, conductors, performers—stop quaking around the periphery of social issues and start promoting the idea that the arts should reflect the human condition," emphasizes Camphouse, who currently serves as professor of music and director of bands at Virginia's Radford University. "Too often, we in the arts community are perceived as being off in our own little worlds.

"And, don't get me wrong. It's okay for artists to nurture their creative impulses and refine their technique. But there needs to be a balance that includes being an involved citizen, especially during these harrowing times of shrinking arts budgets and shrinking dollars for arts education."

So Camphouse unpeels multiple layers of the arts in his composing, conducting, and playing. They include ever-present social issues; the fight for government funding of the arts; keen attention to perfecting musical textures, colors, and rhythm; as well as being a spokesman for the arts as an integral part of academics.

One of his role models is Bruno Walter, who, in his book *Of Music and Musicmaking*, wrote, "A musician who calls himself only a musician is only half a musician."

For someone who has had no direct contact with the problem of child abuse, Camphouse was moved by the frightening statistics and reports that crop up every day in the media. In 1993, he was commissioned by the conductor of the St. Louis Youth Wind Ensemble to compose a piece that would call attention to a current problem or injustice.

The title, "Watchman, Tell Us of the Night," was inspired by a different setting of the Thanksgiving hymn, "Come, Ye Thankful People, Come." Although his work is purely instrumental, the entire verse inspired his composing.

"I attempt to portray the feelings of an abused child without giving an overt description of abuse," notes the multidimensional composer. "I chose not to take the easy way out and get in the listener's face with a lot of dissonance.

"Instead, this single-movement work is very subtle. I aim to convey the anguishing aloneness, lost innocence, yet hope of the child survivor. It, therefore, ends unresolved. It fades away—goes off into infinity—because this is a continuing problem."

Responding to cuts in arts programs across our nation's schools, he encourages parents to involve their children in the arts to instill in them, at an early age, not only an appreciation but an understanding that the arts overlap in all aspects of life.

For More Information

American Symphony Orchestra League
910 Seventeenth Street NW
Washington, DC 20006
www.symphony.org

American Guild of Organists
475 Riverside Drive, Suite 1260
New York, NY 10115
www.agohq.org

Chamber Music America
305 Seventh Avenue, Fifth Floor
New York, NY 10001
www.chamber-music.org

National Association of Schools of Music
11250 Roger Bacon Drive, Suite 21
Reston, VA 22091
www.arts-accredit.org

Opera America
1156 Fifteenth Street NW, Suite 810
Washington, DC 20005
www.operaam.org

CHAPTER FIVE

Careers in Opera

In Edith Wharton's *The Age of Innocence*, New York's self-appointed aristocrats of good taste welcomes the opera season, in the early part of the twentieth century, with the same enthusiasm and respect they would accord visiting dignitaries. Emulating a distinctly European tradition, America's upper classes basically set the long-held standard that opera is an elitist art form. Today, with top ticket prices of two hundred dollars and up, that theory still seems to ring true.

However, world-class and small, professional opera companies exist that offer blocks of tickets in the more affordable range. Moreover, the stars themselves come from diverse backgrounds. And opportunities abound for roles in local operatic and musical theatre productions, symphonic concerts and recitals, and music festivals.

While there is still a very specific die-hard opera audience, the variety of operatic expression is attracting a more eclectic following. Romantic classics, such as Verdi's *La Traviata*, Puccini's *La Boheme*, and Bizet's *Carmen*, reach diverse listeners. On the other hand, Wagner's three-part *Ring Cycle*, Phillip Glass's minimalist style, and William Bolcom's dissonance demand an acquired taste. The field is still evolving, and there is great demand for opera around the world. It can't be denied that the art form has a concentrated contingent of loyal devotees.

Opera singers fall in the music category, along with musical directors, accompanists, and prompters. But because of the specific requirements of the discipline, this chapter examines opera in more depth.

Opera Singers

Like other singers, as discussed in Chapter 4, opera singers also must interpret music using their knowledge of voice production, melody, and tonal structure. They are categorized according to their vocal range—soprano, mezzo-soprano, contralto, tenor, baritone, or bass. A key distinction for opera singers is that they are required to master the many languages in which they sing (most notably Italian, German, French, and English). And they are grandiose actors who create intense characterizations that appear larger than life on stage. The art form demands exaggeration and its fair share of melodrama.

Opera singers often begin vocal instruction at an early age before moving on to advanced music or voice degree programs at the college or university level. If you are serious about tackling opera as a profession, you must be vigilant about protecting your voice. Wearing scarves and wraps to guard against cold drafts is standard practice, as is drinking warm tea flavored with honey to lubricate the vocal chords.

Practice is constant, as are travel and long, erratic rehearsals. Performances can last from two to five hours—or, if you are doing *The Ring Cycle*, days! Getting into and out of your elaborate costumes and makeup can take hours, too. Baritone and opera/musical theatre star Robert Goulet commented that when he performed in *Man of La Mancha*, it took two showers to wash the white powder dye out of his hair. Then he had to put it on again the next day—sometimes for two performances.

Musical Directors

The role of a musical director for opera is similar to that of an artistic director and conductor. Musical directors coordinate programming, hold auditions, and lead rehearsals. Their background is classical music, with an emphasis on the operatic canon. They also must have a flair for the theatrical. Many musical directors conduct the orchestra in musical theatre productions.

Like their singers, they are intimately acquainted with the language and style of the work they are presenting. Musical directors must be able to take charge, have dynamic personalities, and display vibrant organizational skills. Musical directors must create harmony among the egos, too—prima donnas and temperamental tenors are still part of the legendary theatrics.

Accompanists and Prompters

Crucial behind-the-scenes opera occupations are accompanist and prompter. During the long rehearsal periods—and equally long coaching sessions—piano accompanists are indispensable to the singers. They provide the basic melodies, which performers master. To hire a full orchestra for each rehearsal would be cost prohibitive. Therefore, skilled accompanists are able to re-create the score as close as possible to orchestral sound—without incurring exorbitant fees.

A thorough knowledge of tempo, melody, and tonal structure is required. Accompanists often become an extension of the singers—carrying them through the proper beats and pacing of classic arias.

If you have ever wondered what that little domed box, dead center, on the stage's floor is used for, here's the answer. A prompter, or specialist in vocal cues and musical arrangements, is stationed below it (hidden from the audience's view). The prompters guide the singers through their complex solos and duets. But they don't exactly mouth the words to them. Instead, prompters "conduct" the vocalists—giving them the correct tempo signals and subtly sending key introductory passages in their fairly close direction.

Both professions involve intense training in the mechanics of music and voice.

Getting Started

Receiving proper training from seasoned professionals is the best starting point for all performing artists. Opera is no exception. By joining forces with an outstanding instructor, you will have streamlined access to some of the most significant vocal competitions, advanced study programs, and career-launching performance opportunities available.

Singing in the shower also may not be a bad place to begin. The trick is being able to transform those private solos into booming performances for the masses. You should audition for as many school musicals or operettas as possible to get a sense of what's expected of you. Learn a variety of roles, from choral and character parts to leads. In order to develop a style you are comfortable with—and to mature as an artist—strive to perform frequently before an audience. Consider singing at weddings or as part of your church choir.

Subscribe to an opera or operetta series and attend pre- or post-show lectures and backstage tours. Read the artists' biographies in the programs to become familiar with the profession's general career path. If you just want to experience the grandeur of an opera production without having to sing, try out for supernumerary, or "extra," roles. You get to rehearse with the cast, wear a costume, and provide an animated backdrop (as in crowd scenes). Occasionally, you may get a chance to interact with performers.

Musical directors often gain early experience by directing musicals and classical concerts at schools, music conservatories, or local opera troupes. Accompanists and prompters can also hone their skills in school settings by taking part in show rehearsals.

Educational and Apprenticeship Requirements

Opera is a specialized field of music that requires singers to perfect their instruments through constant private instruction and study at institutions of higher learning. The music field still promotes old-world methods of mentor-student training. An audition is generally required for entry into a formal music or voice program.

Courses for opera singers are much the same as they are for musicians: voice theory and instruction (with an emphasis on proper breathing techniques), as well as music interpretation, composition, and history.

Musical directors take a wide range of music and conducting courses, and accompanists and prompters receive a solid instrumental and voice education.

Many colleges, universities, and music conservatories grant bachelor's or higher degrees in music. They combine theory and performance. A vital supplement to any opera or music education is studying abroad with master teachers.

Finding a Job in Opera

Rising through the ranks is a familiar method of advancement in opera. Landing a position in an opera chorus prepares singers for the intricate dynamics involved in working together on stage with a large cast. It is also an excellent opportunity to observe star performers in action. Some singers prefer participating in classical or symphonic recitals.

If the thought of finding work on your own—in such a specialized field—seems daunting to you, hire an agent who works with an artists' management firm. Agents are tapped into the classical music scene. They can match the job openings with your level of skill, talent, look, and stage presence. In addition, they negotiate contracts and can manage your publicity.

Musical directors, accompanists, and prompters keep their ears open for available positions with orchestras and opera companies. Information is consistently exchanged between music schools and the concert stage. By pursuing a music degree at a reputable institution, you will learn about plenty of performing opportunities.

Word travels fast from the stage to the wings and to the conservatory classroom.

Salary and Success Outlook for Opera Professionals

Opera singers usually belong to a branch of the American Guild of Musical Artists. Competition for opera jobs is acute. Therefore, talent and marketing savvy are needed to make major career strides. Agents negotiate contracts, with earnings varying tremendously—from chorus members earning $200 per week to multimillionaire stars. Many opera singers supplement their on-stage pay with royalties from classical recordings they have made. Recording is a highly lucrative business in opera.

Earnings often depend on a performer's professional reputation, place of employment, and the number of hours worked. The basic salary range is anywhere from $200 to $600 a week, depending on the size of the company and its success at the box office. The most successful artists earn far more than the minimum, which is approximately $1,000 per week for singers working in New York.

Musical directors, accompanists, and prompters work out contracts with their unions. They focus on the number of weeks in an opera season, rehearsal schedules, and number of performances.

Interviews with Opera Singers

The following profiles originally appeared in Pioneer Press newspaper articles by the author. They offer information on the career paths taken by two internationally renowned opera singers and are reprinted here with permission.

....

Baritone David Holloway

Baritone David Holloway has been performing nonstop throughout the United States and Europe for close to forty years.

"Singing should be as natural as it possibly can be," says Holloway. "One should emulate a baby's cry; to achieve this, infants
use their whole body. This idea illustrates breath and its connection to voice."

But that's where the theorizing stops. Holloway, who prefers to
demonstrate techniques rather than overanalyze them, promotes
an old-fashioned teaching style that allows students to find their
own individual sounds. Throughout his training, he preferred
teachers who—in addition to providing solid technique—gave
him a hint, then let him discover his unique form of artistic
expression.

"I liked to absorb as much as I could very quickly," recalls Holloway, a Kansas native. "Yet, I learned one of the most valuable
lessons of my career when I studied voice in Italy with Maestro
Ricci, who taught me to slow down and experience the depth of
each note and characterization."

Over the course of his vast and varied vocal career, Holloway
found that his repertoire continued to expand as he grew as a person. Although he began singing at the age of three and has studied piano since the age of five, the affable artist did not consider
an operatic singing career until he entered Kansas University,
where he received both a bachelor's and a master's degree in voice.

He spent six seasons with the Kansas City Lyric Opera before
debuting with the Lyric Opera of Chicago in Britten's *Billy Budd*
in 1970 and at the New York City Opera in Mozart's *Cosi Fan Tutte*
two years later. His impressive career includes seven seasons with
New York's Metropolitan Opera.

"I actually wanted to be an actor and somehow fell into voice," quips Holloway, who is thinking of taking classes in Shakespearean theatre. "I was fortunate to have performed in the more intimate European theatres—1,350 seats, for example—that prevented me from exaggerating.

"Most of the stage directors there come from the theatre. Consequently, they pushed very hard to train us in creating characterizations from within while eliminating the extraneous gestures."

Performing in Europe also gave Holloway an opportunity to delve more deeply into opera, which is a distinctly European art form. He relished the seven-week rehearsal periods that devoted the first two weeks exclusively to the music—unlike the quick musical run-throughs often done in the United States. And he worked on one production at a time, versus jumping around to different singing engagements simultaneously.

"That's not to say I disapprove of opera in the United States," Holloway adds. "I've found that when companies here pride themselves in featuring stars, something gets lost—after all, stars don't rehearse. You have to come out of an ensemble situation to reap the benefits of rehearsing together and better understanding the subtleties of the music."

The singer lived and worked for ten years in Dusseldorf, Germany, where he was principal baritone in the ensemble of the Deutsche Oper am Rhein. His repertoire included Figaro in *Il Barbiere di Siviglia*; Figaro and Count Almaviva in *Le Nozze di Figaro*; Giovanni in *Don Giovanni*; Scarpia in *La Tosca*; and the title leads in *Onegin*, *Julius Caesar*, and *Rigoletto*.

Holloway made it a point to master German, Italian, and French in order to more completely elicit "the idiosyncrasies of character and the hidden meanings of curious idiomatic expressions." A traditionalist at heart, he seeks the "pure innards of music."

His current interest in Shakespearean drama, with its "length, depth, and tremendous weight of the language," flows quite naturally from his lifelong work in opera.

How has he managed to perform regularly, with only one or two minor colds getting in the way?

"I was never obsessed with protecting my voice," explains Holloway. "I've led a very healthy life, have been doing yoga for over twenty years, and I come from Kansas—what else can I tell you?"

Mezzo-Soprano Florence Quivar

Mezzo-soprano Florence Quivar doesn't just live to sing. She sings to live—and touch the lives of as many listeners as possible. To help achieve that, she opts for the highly accessible "symphonic concert" venue.

"I'm looking for longevity in my singing, and I feel that I can have a longer and healthier career—and reach more people—by performing symphonic works," she explains.

Additionally, this arrangement allows the Philadelphia-born artist to bring her own depth and spontaneity to a musical work that she says "changes with each performance."

Well known to New York audiences, the charismatic vocalist has graced the Metropolitan Opera House stage for several seasons, performing in *Oedipus Rex, Don Carlo, Luisa Miller, Porgy and Bess, Siegfried, Un Ballo in Maschera*, and many more.

Nevertheless, recitals are her preference.

Admitting that in Verdi, for instance, the "mezzo-soprano does all the ugly character parts," Quivar has often found herself in a paradoxical position. She mentioned that for a role such as Eboli in *Don Carlo*, her rich melodious voice, while effective, does not project the "biting" or "cutting" sound required.

In a recital atmosphere, the dynamic operatic talent can sing concert versions of *Aida* and do a delicious smorgasbord of Mahler that reveals the beauty and vibrancy of her voice. But the candid Quivar notes that the symphonic scene has its drawbacks, too.

"On the concert stage, you stand rigidly in front of the audience. You're out there all by yourself getting all the attention. And, unlike an opera production," she says with a laugh, "you can't turn upstage to a tree if you have to cough."

Fortunately, she's had no vocal tickles during her many performances with the Chicago Symphony Orchestra, Berlin Philharmonic, London Philharmonic, Montreal Symphony, BBC Symphony Orchestra, and Israel Philharmonic, among others.

Quivar also has embarked on a very personal quest to rescue "lost" scores by nineteenth- and twentieth-century African-American composers. Many can be found in libraries, where only the preserved original compositions exist.

"There were a great number of African-American composers who were arranging classical music as well as Negro spirituals," she points out. "It's quite a challenge to get your hands on this music because certain libraries don't even permit photocopies of these scores; many are protected behind glass.

"Yet it remains one of my goals to compile a program of these neglected composers and someday record them."

Quivar's easy sense of humor and openness can be traced to her musical childhood. Her mother was a singer, pianist, and organist who taught music at home and brought the joy of song to Philadelphia's Nineteenth Street Baptist Church.

"There always was a variety of music in our house," notes Quivar, a graduate of the Philadelphia Academy of Music and a former member of the Juilliard Opera Theatre. "I find that it is so important for kids today—especially in the public schools—to be exposed to a well-rounded musical education. They can't just know rap music or they will isolate themselves from the bigger picture."

Her advice to aspiring vocalists is equally up-front: "Don't come to New York—it's too expensive to try to live and a get a career going here." But she did recommend being overly prepared and ambitious because the scarcity of jobs makes competition in the performing arts fiercer than ever.

So, what sets someone like Quivar apart from the teeming crowds of vocalists? One of her friends remarked to her after a concert, "Florence, all of the generosity and love you give is in your music."

For More Information

Opera America
1156 Fifteenth Street NW, Suite 810
Washington, DC 20005
www.operaam.org

National Association of Schools of Music
11250 Roger Bacon Drive, Suite 21
Reston, VA 22091
www.arts-accredit.org

CHAPTER SIX

Opportunities in Theatrical Design

Imagine for a moment a production of Arthur Miller's *Death of a Salesman* or Broadway musicals such as *Thoroughly Modern Millie*, *Rent*, or *Hairspray* without any scenery or costumes. What a grave disappointment that would be. After all, it is through the stage's overall design that audiences become truly immersed in the essence of the work being staged.

Theatrical design cuts across all areas of the performing arts and increasingly involves intense collaboration among its team members. Illustrative of this magical combination is the 1977 dance film *The Turning Point*, in which Ann Bancroft (as an aging ballerina) describes how all the pain and hard work were worth it when the lights, costumes, music, and sets all came together on stage.

The vast area of design has a fascinating history, dating back to Elizabethan times. Scenic designers come from diverse backgrounds, ranging from art, architecture, computer graphics, interior design, and theatre. Some of them are also lighting and sound designers—subcategories that naturally go together. Others add costume design, which combines experience in fashion with the theatrical profession.

In the performing arts arena, designers are employed by a theatre, opera, or dance company as residents, or they work on special commissions as freelancers. Advances in technology have made computer designs the current and future industry standard of operation. Even costume designers are using computers to format and cut patterns—a technique that is rapidly replacing hand sketching and stitching. Working closely with designers are properties masters and backstage dressers, both vital assistants to the smooth onstage running of a production.

History of Theatrical Design

The theatrical designers' plight for recognition is embodied in the history of the United Scenic Artists Union (Local 829). It began to organize during a time when designers created, built, and painted their own scenery; actors provided their own costumes; and lighting was achieved with gaslight.

In September 1895, the original Scenic Artists Union, known as the Protective Alliance of Scenic Painters of America, was founded as National Alliance of Theatrical Stage Employees Local 38. The Alliance of Scenic Artists struggled for twenty-two years to gain nationwide acceptance as a bona fide union. But its charter was revoked by the American Federation of Labor (AFL) when its scenic painting jurisdiction was claimed by the Brotherhood of Painters, Decorators, and Paper Hangers (another AFL union).

The Alliance persisted in trying to be recognized by the AFL until June 1918, when the Scenic Artists were granted a charter as an autonomous local of the Brotherhood of Painters, Decorators, and Paper Hangers. To this day, the Scenic Artists remain an autonomous local of this brotherhood, which is now known as the Brotherhood of Painters and Allied Trades.

In the early 1920s, scenic designers were brought into Local 829 as members. In the 1930s, costume designers, mural artists, diorama and display workers, and makeup artists were given associate member status. Finally, in the 1950s, lighting designers were included as associate members.

From twenty members in 1895 to close to three thousand today, Local 829 has become a nationwide local of scenic artists, as well as costume and lighting designers, for every type of theatre, dance, opera, film, television, and live advertising venture (such as commercials) throughout the United States. It has negotiated agreements with the League of American Theatres, the League of Regional Theatres, numerous scenery supply companies, the Metropolitan Opera, regional opera and ballet companies, major film studios, television networks, and many independent production companies.

Local 829's scenic artists and craftspeople bring their designers' visions to life, whether the vision is a re-creation of Vietnam (real helicopters and all) in *Miss Saigon*, a sensually ornate Arabic backdrop for the ballet *La Bayadere*, a smoky nineteenth-century Parisian garret in the opera *La Boheme*, or a vintage 1940s kitchen from a Frank Gilroy play. Members live in forty-three states and ten other countries. They work in every form of entertainment, from motion pictures in Los Angeles and television in New York to commercials in Chicago, musicals in St. Louis, opera in Santa Fe, and drama in Seattle. Local 829's main office is in New York, with regional branches in Chicago, Los Angeles, and Miami.

Scenic Designers

As part of the production team, scenic designers confer with directors, actors, and their artistic colleagues on the look, mood, or ambience of a show. They design the sets for live theatrical productions as well as movies and television shows. The focus here is on those who design for live stage events.

In order to create effective and evocative backdrops, scenic designers must study scripts and work together with directors, who describe their own personal design vision. Scenic designers then produce sketches or scale models to guide construction of the actual sets. They also conduct extensive research, especially if the work is an eighteenth-century farce, a Shakespearean adaptation, or one of the endless period plays, operas, and ballets in the performing arts canon.

The pace of production moves very rapidly, so scenic designers are often under pressure to make quick and last-minute changes. Expect long, indeterminate hours spent designing, building, and researching. You will also want to make it a point to visit flea markets and garage sales for the necessary materials and vintage items critical to authentic stage sets.

Lighting Designers

The majority of lighting designers agree that the most effective lighting is the unobtrusive, or unnoticeable, kind because it complements—rather than detracts from—the action on stage. That theory probably accounts for the widespread "invisibility" of lighting designers, who are crucial partners to the scenic, sound, and costume artists. It is frequently the lighting designer who accentuates pivotal moments in a show capable of eliciting a strong emotional response from the audience.

As master technicians, lighting designers must have extensive knowledge of massive, computerized light boards and programming systems. Their cues correspond with key moments in the script, making their job akin to choreographing with colors, shadows, and dramatic half-lights. They work very hard to achieve the desired illumination effects, and they are sensitive to the way lights bounce off actors' faces and the sets that surround them. It's amazing how lighting can totally alter the look of an actor or place.

As expected, lighting designers must be team players willing to work long, sporadic hours. And they must be prepared for any last-minute changes. Since they are working with electrical equipment, they have to be diligent in their safety efforts. Checking for frayed wires and short currents is mandatory. Working with complicated electrical equipment comes with a responsibility to make sure it is all in top-notch condition. Creating a safe environment is paramount.

Sound Designers

Like their lighting counterparts, sound designers work with computerized electrical equipment that must be constantly monitored for safety. A microphone improperly grounded can electrocute the person who picks it up. But, fervent safety warnings aside, sound design is also an intricate art form essential to the movement of a staged work.

Sound designers develop the aural, or sound, cues crucial to a play's mood. Running water, traffic, the murmuring of a crowd, or strains of music are the kinds of sound effects used as an integral part of a production. They should blend seamlessly with the stage action.

The sound aspect of this business became wildly popular during the golden age of radio when sound designers were called Foley artists. They also integrated sound effects into film and, to this day, hold jobs in the motion picture and radio industries, where radio versions of plays are coming back in vogue. Jobs, however, are scarce these days for Foley artists. Therefore, these resourceful designers can be found more frequently backstage marrying their love of theatre with their unique sensitivity toward sound.

Interview with Sound Designers

Following are excerpts from an interview the author conducted with prolific Chicago sound designers Andre Pluess and Ben Sussman for *Stage Directions* magazine.

Andre Pluess and Ben Sussman regularly go out on aural scavenger hunts. Pluess might ask his collaborator to call him and let the answering machine pick up so he can record the beep. They suspend microphones over congested intersections or near running water to capture a kaleidoscope of natural sound fragments. They later shape these snippets into an evocative landscape for one of the myriad productions they are working on.

The Chicago-based composers and sound designers—who work more often as a team than separately—are changing the way local theatres approach sound. Forget standard reactive tactics, like the ubiquitous doorbell or gunshot. Pluess and Sussman create a sound palette that illuminates the mood and theme of a script. They often team up with progressive companies that take a multidisciplinary approach to theatre.

"We're most successful when we try to integrate as many audible elements into the act of storytelling as possible," says Pluess, "like music, ambient sound, voiceovers, or live actor-generated sound."

Perhaps it was their broad backgrounds that helped mold their all-encompassing ear for sound design. Pluess and Sussman met at the University of Chicago while writing music for the student-run University Theatre. Both multi-instrumentalists since young ages, they composed pieces for a gamut of theatrical genres ranging from Shakespeare to avant-garde performance art.

Interestingly, neither pursued a music or technical major. Sussman, who majored in mathematics, graduated in 1994—one year ahead of Pluess, who holds a degree in European church history. This rather unconventional blend of musical, scientific, and historic expertise proved an advantage as they found themselves in demand for devising the sonic backdrop for the University Theatre's vast scope of shows.

The designers describe their process.

"First it's about reading the play," explains Pluess. "Then it's about hearing the play. An automatic genesis of aural ideas sets in motion the instrumental vocabulary of the piece. It's more of a gut connection of what we envision as a vocabulary of sounds."

Continues Sussman, "Sound becomes part of the image. Different theatres have different trademarks. Lookingglass always works in a heightened reality. Once we know what the role of sound is—narrative, supportive, transitional—then it's a question of jumping in. We start recording and laying out tracks, followed by the tech process: the integration of prerecorded elements into the show."

Each designer has a home studio. Their equipment of choice includes a Kurzweil digital piano, Mackie mixers, AKG and Shure microphones, an Alesis external effects generator, a PC version of the Pro-Audio 9 computer program, and MIDI disks for playbacks.

Costume Designers

As a costume designer, you will be working with unusual fabrics and styles—many that mirror the period of the production at hand. Therefore, in-depth research into the cuts, patterns, and materials used throughout history is a natural aspect of your job. Also, remember that you are designing clothes that must be seen from a great distance by an audience. Construct your garments on a large scale, and become familiar with using durable thread, which lessens the wear-and-tear of these costumes.

If you are attracted to dramatic theatre, opera, music, or dance from a behind-the-scenes perspective, and you are a talented artist, then a career in costume design could be very rewarding. You will most likely work in a spacious studio, where you sketch ideas before cutting out a pattern. You will then spend time searching for rare combinations of fabrics at garage sales, flea markets, or thrift shops.

The rest of your time will include costume fittings with performers, sewing and making alterations, and long hours in rehearsal to get a clear idea of the show's mood and how the actors and directors are interpreting it.

Getting Started in Theatrical Design

If you have a flair for interior design, are attracted to art and architecture, and are technically adept, you can get a head start in the scenic and lighting design industry by working as an artisan's apprentice. Furniture makers and fabric designers can teach you the rudiments of design, and getting a part-time job at a showroom for household accoutrements would give you a hands-on opportunity to experience the interplay of light, textures, and objects.

These basic skills transfer positively to theatre, where rooms, destinations—and worlds—are created on stage to evoke a mood or idea or to transport the audience to a certain time and place. Once you have mastered the basics, you can assist with a community or school production or help with special events requiring decor (such as a fund-raising fashion or variety show or neighborhood festival).

Sound designers have a natural sensitivity to the nuances of rhythm, percussion, and melody. They enjoy molding noises into recognizable images. They are typically die-hard music fans with eclectic and experimental tastes. Working in radio or for a studio that dubs sound cues in music could provide excellent experience. Computer know-how is essential, as well as solid technical capabilities. Employment at an electronic and/or musical instrument store or repair shop will familiarize you with the basic components of sound equipment.

Then, if theatre intrigues you, hook up with a company in the same way scenic and lighting designers would. Actually, all three areas are interconnected. Many sound designers also do lighting or a little bit of everything. Hands-on experience builds confidence with the wide-ranging—and increasingly high-tech—equipment and materials that are their tools of the trade.

Two of the best places to test your costume design talents are in high school or with a local community theatre group. Both will give you the opportunity to create the look of small-scale shows and will familiarize you with the general workings of the theatrical world. Take basic sewing and design courses to sharpen your hand-stitching and pattern-cutting skills. Practice sketching, which is another vital aspect of this profession.

Then spend time in the library or a museum researching period costume fabrics, design, and construction. It also wouldn't hurt to take acting and scenic design courses to learn how to work within other disciplines of the theatre.

In addition, you can prepare by going to a lot of live shows and to the movies for a basic understanding of trends, techniques, and types of costumes needed. In your spare time, visit costume shops and clothing boutiques to see how these specialized items are constructed.

Finally, get out to see as many theatrical performances and movies as you can to observe trends and unique, intriguing design concepts.

Educational and Apprenticeship Requirements

The National Association of Schools of Art and Design has accredited about two hundred postsecondary institutions with programs in art and design, most of which award a degree in art or design. Many schools do not allow formal entry into a bachelor's degree program until a student has successfully finished a year of basic art and design courses. Applicants may be required to submit sketches and other examples of their artistic abilities.

Two- and four-year degree programs in fine arts exist throughout the United States, as well as two- and three-year professional schools that award certificates or associate degrees in design. The Foundation for Interior Design Education Research also accredits interior design programs and schools. Currently, there are more than 120 accredited professional programs in the United States and Canada, primarily located in schools of art, architecture, and home economics.

Interviews with Theatrical Designers

As part of a special design-education issue of *PerformInk*, a Chicago-based arts industry trade publication, the author interviewed a wide spectrum of designers who shared their input on training programs and gave some honest advice on job opportunities. Excerpts are reprinted here with permission.

Liberal arts colleges have been touting the benefits of a "well-rounded" education for eons. And they must be on to something, since local scenic, lighting, costume, and sound designers are promoting the same all-encompassing philosophy.

"Theatre people are citizens of the world," says John Musial, known for his audience-integrated sets—many for Lookingglass Theatre. "And their work should reflect life experiences."

As an undergraduate theatre major at Northwestern University, Musial satisfied his acting, theatre history, and technical credits while emphasizing all aspects of design. He also broadened his curriculum by taking, for instance, Russian literature and science courses. He points out that a lot of his ideas for incorporating the audience into his sets arose from Northwestern University's Performance Studies Department, which "explores the ritual of performance, rather than acting."

The bulk of theatrical designers interviewed received a degree on the undergraduate or graduate levels related to their fields. Many B.A. or B.F.A. degrees include more general theatre studies, while M.F.A. degrees address specific areas of study, such as scenic design. An overall recommendation is to spend much time working on productions at school and to complete the required amount of courses before venturing into outside projects that can hinder your progress.

"One of the first things you need to learn is how to say no," recommends lighting designer David Gipson. "Your professors will tell you that their course work should be your first priority, then the director of a production you're lighting says it's your first priority. It's important to find that balance and sort out your priorities so that you can devote proper attention to each project."

Because the lighting comes together in a short amount of time during "tech week," Gipson tells design students to stay calm during a crisis: "If you panic, you'll lose control of the lighting design, which is a key visual element that serves to enrich the script's message."

Gipson received his B.F.A. in theatrical design from the University of Texas at Austin, which he notes had "five well-equipped technical facilities that were better than what I found in the real world." That's a key point, since many professionals are often faced with the creative challenge of designing shows within a limited or non-existent budget.

As a sound designer for WNEP Theatre, Don Hall, who is forced to work within a slim budget, has literally created his effects from "things I found in the garbage." Instead of relying on pre-recorded sound effects, he prefers to create his own on stage—à la Foley style—and has done so through trial and error.

Just saying no to an unmanageable array of design projects during college does not necessarily apply to your career life after graduation. According to Musial, since most designers are freelancers, they have to acquire an "inability to say no" when job opportunities arise. "There are so few out there, once you're discovered—even if it means doing jobs for little or no pay—you could have steady work for a long time."

For scenic and lighting designer Chris Phillips, being accepted into the United Scenic Artists Union (Local 829) has not only opened up the doors for more work, but has provided him with substantial benefits.

"Because it's pretty rare for someone to be a resident designer for a Chicago theatre company, it can get disheartening trying to find work as a freelancer," points out Phillips, who holds a B.A. in theatre from Loyola University of Chicago and an M.F.A. in scenic design and technical direction from Detroit's Wayne State University. "To avoid getting abused financially, I applied to a union."

The application to United Scenic Artists includes a take-home project and a portfolio review of design work the applicant has done. Once accepted by a committee, members have access to affordable health insurance, 401(k) plans, inexpensive credit cards, legal help, and salary negotiations.

Teaching at the university level is another way for designers to earn a steady income while continuing to freelance. Costume designers Nan Cibula-Jenkins and Nan Zabriskie are instructors at DePaul University's Theatre School.

Interestingly, both received their bachelor's degrees in non-theatrical fields—history and science. After a chance meeting with a costume designer in a New York hair salon, Cibula-Jenkins decided to enroll at the Yale School of Drama, where she studied all aspects of design, including lighting and sets. Zabriskie realized how much she enjoyed sewing costumes; she received an M.F.A. in theatrical design from the University of Minnesota—another well-rounded program.

"Because you collaborate with other designers, you must speak your team's language," explains Cibula-Jenkins. "It's a real cross-over of information."

Even scenic and lighting designer Phillips acknowledges that "a designer is very dependent on the support he or she gets from the crew, stage manager, assistants, and the theatre's business office. Never be closed to a suggestion."

Cibula-Jenkins also recommends networking and getting out to see as many productions as humanly possible: "Often young designers forget about the community around them; you need a lot of stamina to get yourself known."

Zabriskie agrees, adding that costume designers must have tremendously good people skills, along with good research and drawing talents and a significant knowledge of materials, makeup, prosthetics, and hat- and mask-making techniques."

Her main advice to costume design students is to "get out there and start putting in time."

Adds Cibula-Jenkins, "Costume designers must remember that analysis of the script is very important. Unlike fashion, where making a saleable product is the main goal, costume design is about artistic, three-dimensional sculpture that represents the mood of a play."

Phillips is quick to note that it usually takes about five years for people to think of—and hire—someone as a designer. Then he suggests that "listening, communicating, thinking ahead, and self-motivation" are essential skills for all theatrical designers.

John Culbert, dean of DePaul University's Theatre School and a scenic/lighting designer, stresses that aspiring designers should select a college program that matches their own personal goals: "Don't just go to a school because it has a good reputation—find the right one for you."

Culbert goes a step beyond the liberal arts theory to emphasize what's necessary for survival: "Talent is not the main ingredient for success as a theatrical designer; you need to have determination, drive, and self-discipline."

The Appendix lists educational programs that offer courses in both the performance and technical spheres of theatre arts.

Salary and Success Outlook for Theatrical Designers

Designers held approximately 492,000 jobs in 2000. About one-third were self-employed—a much higher proportion than in most occupations. Median annual earnings for theatre designers were $31,440 in 2000. The middle 50 percent earned between $21,460 and $42,800 a year. The lowest 10 percent earned less than $13,820, while the highest 10 percent earned more than $57,400.

Costume designers employed by a ballet, opera, or theatrical company would start at an annual salary in the mid to high teens, with the possibility of advancing to the high thirties and forties. It is difficult to give a general pay scale because costume design work is often sporadic and seasonal. Some of the best rewards are intangible, focusing more on artistic achievement and recognition than on high pay and bonuses.

There are also the few legendary exceptions to the rule—big-time costume designers whose work is so extraordinary, they earn profits in the millions. However, most costume designers will tell you that their incomes are modest, but their jobs are fun and fulfilling.

Many talented individuals are attracted to careers as designers. Consequently, designers in most fields can expect to face competition throughout their careers. Due to this competition, individuals with little or no formal education in design, and without the necessary personal traits (particularly creativity and perseverance), may find it very difficult to establish and maintain a career in design.

Employment in design occupations is expected to grow faster than the average for all occupations through 2010. Growth in population and in personal incomes is expected to encourage increased demand for theatrical designers. In addition to employment growth, many job openings will result from the need to replace designers who leave the field.

Properties Masters and Dressers

Properties masters work hand-in-hand with scenic designers to find or create the actual props used in a production. Sofas, beds, tables, chairs, lamps, dishes, and automobiles create a mood or setting the same way backdrops and costumes do. They all join together like a symphony, harmoniously blending colors, patterns, and textures.

During performances, properties masters supervise the black-bedecked crew members who move the props around during scene changes. They also keep track of objects, which they catalog and keep in good working condition.

Flea markets, garage sales, and vintage stores are properties masters' best friends. Properties masters are even known to scour alleys where a discarded desk or ottoman may add the perfect touch to a set. If you already collect memorabilia—or consider yourself a pack rat, capable of making worn antiques look like artistic masterpieces—you may be well suited to a very unique, but little known, career as a properties master.

Considered unsung heroes of the theatrical profession, back-stage dressers make all those quick costume changes seem effortless. If you are interested in this rarely publicized occupation, try to attend a production of Ronald Harwood's play, *The Dresser*, which meticulously reveals the codependent relationship between an aging actor/manager and his dresser/factotum. It powerfully explores how the title character desperately seeks approval in an occupation that demands attentiveness but fosters invisibility.

Despite that slightly melodramatic description, backstage dressers are not necessarily desperate people. However, their profession is one of long hours, assorted egos, and very little recognition.

Besides helping performers get in and out of their costumes at rapid-fire speed, they also wash and repair these costumes and have mastered the intricate mechanics of working with archaic clothing, including tightly laced corsets, spats, and enormous hoop skirts.

There is more in this unpredictable profession than simply helping actors with costume changes and alterations. You must never succumb to panic and always be resourceful. After all, on average, a quick change can last anywhere from twenty seconds to two minutes—and timing is everything. You also have to deal with long, erratic show-business schedules.

Although theatrical dressers in this country date back to vaudeville, they became firmly established as a profession in the 1940s. In Chicago, for example, the first Theatrical Wardrobe Union was founded in 1943 and consisted mainly of stagehands' wives and cleaning personnel. Today, it is based in Seattle but operates under the umbrella of the New York–based International Alliance of Theatrical Stage Employees.

Because you will be dressing both unknown supporting actors and famous celebrities, be prepared to deal with any personality type. At times, you may even be sought out for advice or to act as a surrogate parent to the complex artists who make up the eclectic theatrical profession.

Getting Started

Properties masters are closely linked to scenic designers. They have artistic backgrounds and a knack for "antiquing." Working with props is a natural outgrowth of visualizing a theatrical production. Volunteering to locate items for school and community shows will get you started on the right track. Since smaller troupes rarely have large prop budgets, you will be forced to get creative by trudging through flea markets and other cost-effective venues, or by constructing your own objects. As a behind-the-scenes player for a local show, you can hone your organizational skills before moving on to elaborate, pressure-intense productions.

First and foremost, to prepare for a career in theatrical dressing, learn to become a top-notch tailor. That's the basis of your job. Enhance that by being able to do on-the-spot alterations or restyling. Like a typing student, time yourself to see how quickly you can repair, button, and lace hard-to-handle fabrics, such as velvet and burlap. Then get out to the theatre and watch as many shows as you can afford. One way to see a lot of shows free is by volunteering as an usher. Talk with backstage dressers—even ask to work as an apprentice.

As in costume design, get started by dressing performers in your school or community theatre productions, where mistakes are a vital part of the learning process. That way, by the time you get to larger theatres, you will have mastered the split-second timing needed to move the show along flawlessly. Train yourself not to get flustered under pressure. If you remain calm and measured, so will the performer you are dressing.

Because choreography is crucial to the smooth running of any production, learn how to pace yourself and arrange your costumes in sync with the performance as a whole.

Educational and Apprenticeship Requirements

No degrees are required to be a successful properties master or backstage dresser. The former requires an extensive knowledge of theatrical terminology and organization, as well as a keen eye for effective design details. The latter demands intricate hands-on skills. More important than a degree for backstage dressers are quick sewing abilities, which can be acquired through an apprenticeship with an established dresser; practice; and textile courses or workshops.

If you can't break into a theatre immediately, apply for a job at a garment manufacturing firm, where you can hone the tools of your trade. Even work at a dry cleaner can provide you with the experience needed to do all kinds of repairs and alterations. It will also familiarize you with the endless varieties of fabrics.

Finally, rely on your own confidence and talent to get to know actors, directors, designers, and other theatrical dressers. Frequent restaurants or neighborhoods where the artistic community hangs out, and keep up with the top local theatre companies and touring shows in your area.

Finding a Job

Properties masters naturally move right into professional or semi-professional theatre jobs following their work in community or school productions. They essentially come from theatre backgrounds and are active in the field, collaborating with directors and designers. As theatre insiders, they are able to network and learn about several opportunities through word of mouth.

Of course, the only option for backstage dressers is to work backstage or on a movie set. Variations on the theme include special promotions outside theatres that require costume changes, such as fund-raisers that include live entertainment. Fashion shows, too, utilize dressers.

Because theatrical dressers work in such a small, tight-knit profession, their craft is often passed on from generation to generation in families, or mentor to student, and so on. This is one way of ensuring an ongoing, quality line of succession. If you have the skills and decide to pursue this field, humble yourself. Volunteer for backstage work until you get your big break. Think of yourself as taking a career route not much different from that of aspiring stars.

Salary and Success Outlook

As in costume design, it is hard to assess the general pay scale of properties masters because work is often sporadic and seasonal. If they are freelancers, they may work out an hourly or flat-fee pay arrangement. For resident properties masters, a salary can be negotiated. But because earnings are quite low and unpredictable, properties masters typically supplement their incomes with a full- or part-time job unrelated to theatre.

The job outlook for the close-knit profession of backstage dressers is not particularly bright. Multitudes of dressers are not in great, constant demand. And the pay is often minimum wage or slightly higher. Yet it is an exciting profession, with opportunities for growth and satisfaction. If you enjoy the nomadic life, you might want to aim for a job as a full-time dresser for a big touring troupe.

Your earnings are close to those of seamstresses and tailors—around $15,000 to $20,000 annually. You can also supplement your income by doing alterations at a dry cleaner, costume shop, or clothing store. Some unions within the theatrical world provide health and insurance benefits to their members.

Makeup Artists: An Overview

Actors may say they are lured by the smell of the "greasepaint," but makeup artists are really the ones attracted to it more pungently. After all, it's the foundation of their craft. Although they are not designers, makeup artists naturally round out the team of collaborators on a theatrical production. They create makeup, which transforms the actors into characters of all ages, shapes, and looks, as well as other-worldly or unrecognizable beings. Their cosmetic palette ties all the elements of design together, especially lighting and costume design.

More akin to painters and sculptors, they mix colors and a variety of materials (clays and plastics, for instance) to evoke an image—abstract or real. They spend years blending products and inventing new character images—the result of education at a cosmetology institute paired with on-the-job experience and a lot of personal trial and error. They may also have begun work as an apprentice to a wig maker, which is a highly specialized trade.

In addition to serving as a makeup artist for school or local theatrical shows, consider working part-time at a department store's cosmetics counter to learn about contouring and blending techniques, as well as the illusions careful makeup application can create.

Makeup artists traditionally attend a two-year cosmetology program at an institute specializing in makeup application, hairstyling, and wigs. These institutes, which are considered trade schools rather than academic institutions, promote apprenticeships for hands-on experience. Most theatre degree programs at the college and university level offer classes in makeup techniques.

If you move in artistic circles, you will naturally keep up-to-date on upcoming productions and special events (such as industry fund-raiser extravaganzas), where you can assist with the makeup. The only way you get noticed is by constantly putting yourself and your work center stage. The only way you get better is by practicing constantly. Networking should be a top priority.

An effective way of promoting yourself is by sending information about yourself to talent agencies tapped into the local theatre scene. Through them, you can find out about a variety of exciting employment opportunities. Makeup artists are needed when movies are filmed in their cities. Many go on the road with film crews and touring stage-production companies.

Salaries for makeup artists vary greatly, depending on the budgets of theatre companies with which you are working. Large Broadway shows and the Hollywood film industry understandably offer the highest salaries—sometimes escalating into the millions. On average, salaries for makeup artists in the seasonal professional theatre scene range from $12,000 to $30,000 per year. It is not uncommon to be both a makeup artist and a costume designer.

. . . .

For More Information

Foundation for Interior Design Education Research
146 Monroe Center NW, Suite 1318
Grand Rapids, MI 49503
www.fider.org

International Alliance of Theatrical Stage Employees
1430 Broadway, Twentieth Floor
New York, NY 10018
www.iatse-intl.org

National Art Education Association
1916 Association Drive
Reston, VA 20190
www.naea-reston.org

National Association of Schools of Art and Design
11250 Roger Bacon Drive, Suite 21
Reston, VA 20190
www.arts-accredit.org

Theatrical Wardrobe Union Local 887
2800 First Avenue SW, Room 229
Seattle, WA 98121
www.districtone.com

CHAPTER SEVEN

Teaching Opportunities in the Performing Arts

he performing arts are a continuum of knowledge, passed on from mentor to student in a way that hasn't changed much over the centuries. Granted, interactive computer programs on CD-ROMs and audio/videotapes place a distance between teacher and instructee. However, these increasingly technical means of education should be considered supplemental to the important hands-on "human" training necessary to the highly intuitive world of performing arts.

Most artists will tell you that they are constantly learning. On the flip side, artists continually teach—either indirectly through example or as certified instructors at all grade levels, in high schools, colleges, universities, and for special workshop or independent arts center programs.

This chapter brings together in an educational context all the art forms previously discussed. It gives an overview of the endless teaching opportunities available in all areas of the arts and shows how complementary a teaching career is to active performing artists. Flexible schedules allow instructors to continue to pursue their acting, dancing, music, or design careers while passing on a wealth of knowledge and experience to students eager to make their careers as full, balanced, and satisfying as possible.

Acting Instructors

As explored in Chapter 2, actors continue to hone their skills beyond their bachelor's or master's degrees. The more advice they get from professionals, the better prepared they are to tackle a gamut of roles. It's often a given for seasoned, working actors to transfer their outstanding communication skills to the academic realm.

While schools with strong performing arts curricula provide a solid foundation, a workshop environment—featuring master classes taught by top-notch artists—offers students specialized classes—in monologue development, for instance—that help them improve certain nagging weak points.

As an instructor, you can find regular work at local acting centers or in theatrical training programs. As a college or university faculty member in the theatre department, you will help teach and advise the more than fourteen million full-time and part-time students in the United States. In the classroom, you will balance lectures with a lot of interaction and critiquing of students' delivery and oral and physical characterization skills. A significant part of the curriculum involves taking your classes to the theatre and introducing students to actors and the backstage mechanics of a production.

Acting instruction mirrors the diverse, sporadically scheduled performing arts world. Many classes are divided between night and day schedules, with attention paid to "dark" (or closed) theatre nights, concurrent rehearsals, and other performance-related commitments. Outside classroom activities include advising students one-on-one, evaluating their progress, and assisting with workshop or annual gala performances.

Dance Instructors

The role a well-trained, sensitive dance instructor plays in guiding a dancer along a safe, healthy, correct, and productive path cannot be stressed enough. Dancers are like athletes—they are in constant training. If they receive poor training during crucial developmental years, their careers run the risk of being curtailed. Having to retrain and undo bad postural or technique-related habits is twenty times more difficult than starting from scratch with outstanding, trustworthy, in-the-know instructors.

Dance teachers, therefore, come from dance backgrounds. They may or may not have been star performers, but their sound training is intact and they have a gift for passing on knowledge in a firm but nonthreatening manner. A thorough understanding of human anatomy is required in order to describe joint rotation and to prevent injury. Dance teachers are also deeply intuitive, determining the amount of drive and ability their students need in order to make it in this competitive field.

Part psychologists, part parental figures, dance instructors get to know their students' dreams and personalities quite well because of the long hours of practice the dance arena demands. They must know just how far to push students without discouraging them. Tapped into quality dance resources, they are often responsible for setting up top auditions for their students with some of the best dance troupes, as well as providing pivotal career-advancing performance opportunities.

Dance instructors can work in a number of venues: in their own or another dancer's studio, for a major dance company's school, in the dance departments of colleges and universities, and on the dance convention circuit. In addition, private coaching is also common.

Music Teachers

Many musicians earn the bulk of their incomes through teaching music in all academic realms and through private instruction. Performance schedules can be sporadic, and seasonal employment with a band or orchestra may not pay all the bills. The same is true for singers in all categories.

Music teachers, however, should not assume that deft playing ability transfers over to teaching skills. To be successful, instructors must possess the same qualities of teachers in general: patience, confidence, sensitivity, and an almost endless pool of analogies and descriptive terminology. Through encouragement and demanding assignments (appropriate to a student's ability), they help foster the joy, discipline, hard work, and precision akin to a rigorous career in music.

Education in the music field is increasingly moving in the direction of eclectic, multicultural works that stress the fusion of a variety of musical categories and styles.

Design Instructors

Teaching students about scenic, lighting, sound, and costume design and makeup application puts you in a more artistic, participatory realm than your colleagues who teach English, math, and political science. Design instructors work in the art, design, or theatre departments of various academic institutions, or they teach special workshops on a specific area of stagecraft.

They are active participants in their fields, working on school or semiprofessional and professional productions. Their instruction encompasses history, fashion, art, architecture, building techniques, computer and technical proficiency, and theatre-related courses. As expected, academic experiences are richly supplemented by hands-on opportunities to carry a design project from start to finish.

Educational Requirements for Performing Arts Instructors

If you decide to teach on a college or university faculty, you would be required to hold at least a master's degree in any of the performing arts fields: theatre, dance, music, voice, design, or other specializations. Many colleges and universities confer bachelor's or higher degrees in dance through the departments of physical education, music, theatre, or fine arts. Most programs concentrate on modern dance but also offer courses in ballet and classical techniques, choreography, dance history, criticism, physical therapy, and movement analysis.

Completion of a college program in dance and education is essential to qualify for employment as an elementary or high school dance teacher. Colleges, as well as conservatories, require graduate degrees, but performance experience often may be substituted. Studio schools usually require teachers to have experience as performers.

A high number of colleges, universities, and music conservatories grant bachelor's or higher degrees in music. Many also grant degrees in music education to qualify graduates for a state certificate to teach music in an elementary or secondary school.

As a teacher, you should continuously hone your oral and written communication skills and develop an effective style that helps you establish rapport with your students. Be prepared to work in a creatively evolving environment, where you receive little direct supervision.

Finding a Job as a Teacher

Your reputation as a consistently dependable, exceptionally talented performer could spark the interest of performing arts institutions, studios, conservatories, and independent education centers. You may even be asked to teach a master class, which is common in the music industry. Professional musicians critique a student's playing following a performance for a live audience.

Dancers are often invited to teach at a by-audition-only summer program or during a dance convention. Actors and directors devote their time to conducting advanced seminars on several different aspects of their craft. Designers whose work has won critical praise and awards are certainly candidates for teaching positions.

There are so many different paths performers can take. Frequently, they choose to be active artists first and teachers second—after they receive advice to give something back to the artistic community through teaching. Local park districts hire teachers to introduce children and teenagers to the limitless benefits of the arts in their lives.

For beginning instructors, working as a substitute teacher will give you constructive experience without the pressure of a full-time position. This arrangement allows you to test the waters and get a sense of how students respond to your teaching style. If substitute teaching is a positive experience, consider pursuing more full-time work in schools and other educational outlets.

Salary and Success Outlook for Performing Arts Instructors

Even in performing arts instruction, it is difficult to assess earnings due to a seasonal, and variably negotiated, pay structure. Teachers who freelance at workshops are paid a flat fee versus college instructors, who earn a set salary.

At institutions of higher learning, earnings are more established. Faculty in four-year institutions earn higher salaries, on the average, than those in two-year schools. According to a 1999–2000 survey by the American Association of University Professors, salaries for full-time faculty averaged $58,400. Earnings for college faculty vary based on rank and type of institution, geographic area, and field.

Those figures drop slightly when applied to high schools and the fine arts profession, as opposed to higher education programs in law or business. Employment of college and university faculty is expected to increase about as fast as the average for all occupations through the year 2005 as enrollments in higher education increase.

Performing Arts Course Descriptions

To get a feel for the types of performing arts workshop classes being offered, peruse the following general samples.

- **Acting I.** This introduction to acting techniques—getting over fears, relaxing, concentration, focusing on stage and the language of theatre—is based on Viola Spolin's theatre games. The second part of the class extends these introductory exercises to work on sensory perception and imagination, as well as development of the vocal and physical instrument. Exercises are derived from improvisational and Stanislavsky-inspired techniques.
- **Building a Character.** The text from scenes and monologues will be researched to define character. A biography will be created with the missing elements filled in with the imagination, costumes, and props. The class will break down physical and vocal blocks, allowing the text and human beings to begin their chemical process. Some outside research required.
- **Creating a One-Person Show.** This workshop is intended for those who want to perform their own work but don't have a clear process for starting out. And it's for seasoned performers who need a place to "hot house" ideas and inspire themselves toward new work. Develop your own performance piece. Techniques of writing, staging, and performing solo or small group works will be considered.
- **Scene Work and Improvisation.** How does an actor approach a scene simply, truthfully, and spontaneously? In this course, the spontaneity of improvisation is drawn upon to enliven an actor's relationship with scripted material. Approximately half of each class is devoted to poetry and language, improvisation, and theatre games. The other half focuses on scene and/or monologue work. Outside rehearsal by all participants is required for the success of this class.

- **How Not to Audition.** All aspects of the professional audition will be examined and practiced—composing a resume, cold reading, choosing and preparing material, performing material in various situations, and making an effective and lasting impression. Emphasis will be placed on improving the student's individual abilities.
- **Advanced Directing.** This course is designed for those wishing to pursue directing on a professional level. Material to be covered includes the relationship of the director to the actors, designers, playwrights, critics, and audience. The class will culminate with a showcase of student presentations.
- **New Play Development Workshop.** Emerging playwrights and directors can now work on putting a new script on its feet. This workshop allows directors and playwrights to fine-tune the script and get accustomed to the collaborative process. Directors and playwrights may enroll as pairs (preferably) or individually and be paired up by the instructors. At the workshop's conclusion, work is showcased before a live audience.
- **Dance Creation.** Students use structured exercises to create original movement and choreography. Concepts and personal experience become dance.
- **Dance/Theatre.** Explore the boundless possibilities offered by this exciting new synthesis of forms. Activities include movement technique, improv, vocal work, writing, reading, viewing, and discussions to guide participants toward creation of original dance/theatre works.
- **Mask and Puppet Building.** Create your own mask and learn basic skills of puppet building. Participants sculpt and paint, with emphasis on dramatic character.
- **Mime/Movement/Theatre.** This course focuses on mime as a process of re-experiencing unity with the natural world and expressing this unity through the physical plane.

- **Musical Theatre.** This class provides an opportunity for people who have had little or no singing experience to learn the basics of singing on stage. It is also useful for intermediate and advanced singers and actors to learn how to prepare and perform songs as monologues and how to choose and prepare audition material in order to be more effective in the marketplace. This course is especially good for actors interested in pursuing roles in musical theatre or improv groups. Students will learn how to sing with an accompanist, use the voice as a musical instrument, and integrate acting and singing skills. A supportive, built-in audience encourages students to overcome nervousness and gain confidence singing "under pressure." Participants need not have had previous acting training but should be relatively comfortable with their singing voices.
- **Physical Comedy.** Trips and flips, slaps, and falls. Dive headfirst into a world of organized chaos and eccentric acrobatics as actor meets cartoon.
- **Stage Combat and Stunt Movement.** Stage combat is the art of simulating violence for the stage so that it's real for the audience and safe for the actors. Punches, kicks, slaps, throws, and whatever else we can come up with will be taught. A skill vital to actor training.
- **Elizabethan Movement and Style.** Come experience the bawdy life and times of Shakespeare's contemporaries. Learn to walk, talk, dance, and play kings, queens, and the Bard's other legendary characters. A physical six-week introduction to the Shakespearean era.
- **Power Workout for Actors.** A two-hour, twice-a-week intensive workout designed to build an actor's body using a combination of Tai Chi, yoga, and floor exercises. Get in shape, build presence, and become a leaner, meaner—and more powerful—performer.

For More Information

See the Appendix for a full listing of arts education resources.

Association of American Colleges and Universities
1818 R Street NW
Washington, DC 20009
www.aacu-edu.org

American Federation of Teachers (AFL-CIO)
555 New Jersey Avenue NW
Washington, DC 20001
www.aft.org

National Association of Schools of Art and Design
11250 Roger Bacon Drive, Suite 21
Reston, VA 20190
www.arts-accredit.org

CHAPTER EIGHT

Careers in Arts Writing and Publicity

B esides advertising, one of the most successful ways to get the word out about performances, featured performing artists, and other arts-related news is by hiring a publicist, either in-house or as an independent contractor. Publicists exchange information with key members of the arts and entertainment media via news releases, media kits, and e-mail over the Internet. When opening night happens, they are the promotions specialists responsible for bringing in the critics and arts writers (print and broadcast), as well as the voting members of theatrical awards committees. Organizing press conferences and theatre promotional tie-ins at shopping malls and ballparks, for example, are other duties.

Interacting with publicists are the arts journalists and critics, who work in a very close-knit, specialized writing arena. Their lives parallel those of actors, since they are often at rehearsals conducting interviews and reviewing shows nightly (and at matinees), with lightning-quick deadlines (typically that evening or the next morning). If they live in a major theatre city, such as New York, Chicago, or Toronto, critics and arts writers are virtually overwhelmed with deadline-specific performing arts–related stories and reviews. Their social and working lives mesh with the art forms they dauntlessly cover.

Performing Arts Publicists

Performing arts publicists, also called promotional specialists or public relations representatives, work for theatre, opera, and dance companies; symphonies and bands; individual artists; presenters; arts organizations; and any number of associations and academic institutions that promote the arts. They are responsible for channeling crucial information about their clients to the media.

Through public relations, clients can get more substantial press coverage than if they do only advertising. Publicists are sought out for their expertise in "working" the media (sparking their interest in a subject) and, subsequently, getting free coverage for their clients.

Publicists can be self-employed, work for an agency, or be on the staff of a theatre or other arts groups. They often work around the clock in a competitive, fast-paced environment that makes relentless demands on their time and endurance. Most theatrical events take place in the evening and on weekends. Publicists must have outgoing, enthusiastic personalities—and be able to convince the media that the person, group, or company they represent is newsworthy. They must sell constantly, always be on, acquire a sensitivity toward editors' deadlines, and never get discouraged by the sometimes abrupt, curt manner found in the media.

Getting Started

Because the performing arts public relations field requires strong written and verbal communication skills, hone your craft by writing and submitting articles to your school newspaper, and concentrate on public speaking. The debate club is an excellent means for practicing sales techniques, which good publicists must have in order to get the word out on their clients' businesses.

Like the performing artists themselves, publicists find that a good place to get experience is by doing publicity for school and community productions. Work alongside a full-time publicity professional to get the scoop on proper communication tactics to apply toward the often fastidious arts media.

Additionally, read all types of periodicals, watch TV for trends, and get up to speed on the Internet, where publicity is headed throughout the twenty-first century. And, in a world where it's more common to e-mail someone than pick up the phone, do not forget the importance of verbal communication and establishing professional relationships.

Educational Requirements

A college education, combined with public relations experience usually achieved through an internship and work in the performing arts sector, is considered excellent preparation for a career as a performing arts publicist. Most students major in public relations, journalism, advertising, or communication.

Many colleges and universities offer bachelor's and post-secondary degrees in public relations, usually in a journalism or communications department. Common courses are public relations principles and techniques; management and administration, including organizational development; writing news releases, proposals, annual reports, scripts, and speeches; desktop publishing and computer graphics; and research, emphasizing survey design and implementation.

Most colleges are affiliated with companies (including those related to the performing arts) that provide on-the-job internships, for which students apply and go through an extensive interviewing process. Some pay and give college course credit; others just provide the course credit and an impressive addition to your resume.

Getting Hired as a Performing Arts Publicist

As a public relations professional, you do not have to seek employment only in the performing arts realm. On-the-job skills, such as sharp writing and effective communication, apply to a variety of clients. Therefore, you might want to gain some early experience at a public relations agency. If it specializes in creative clients, such as the city's symphony orchestra or a major theatre, all the better. But, even if it does not, you will have a chance to work on a variety of projects, which will prepare you for future promotions-based assignments.

In this competitive business, however, you have to move quickly. If you decide to go it alone and promote yourself as an independent publicist, you should move in prime artistic circles. Make yourself known in the industry. Prove yourself. And speak the language of the art form you are promoting. Attend opening nights, benefits, parties, and other high-profile arts events where the movers and shakers congregate. You should also send a professionally designed and organized information packet about your company to various arts groups and hire someone to design your own website.

Salary and Success Outlook for Performing Arts Publicists

Median annual earnings for salaried public relations specialists were $39,580 in 2000. The middle 50 percent earned between $29,610 and $53,620; the lowest 10 percent earned less than $22,780; and the top 10 percent earned more than $70,480.

Competition among recent college graduates for public relations positions is expected to continue, as the number of applicants will most likely exceed the number of job openings. Degrees are essential, especially in the majors of communication, journalism, public relations, and advertising. People without the appropriate educational background or work experience will face the toughest obstacles in finding a public relations job.

Due to the downsizing of major corporations and decreased government funding of the arts, many public relations specialists are branching out on their own and contracting their services to top clients. Here the competition is fiercer than ever.

Arts Writers and Critics

There's a fascinating yin and yang tugging at combined arts writers and critics. As features writers, they create often flattering stories about upcoming shows and the artists who make them happen. Then, as critics, they must detach themselves from any outside influences and review productions, concerts, and other performances that can range from astounding to dismal. It is their job to judge a work based on high standards of quality and effectiveness, then present a balanced critique pointing out constructively how a show could be more artistically successful.

Therefore, it takes a very confident and democratic individual with an in-depth knowledge of the subject matter to succeed in this limited field. Even in the major arts cities there are only a handful of critics whose words can keep a show running for decades or close it outright. They wield a lot of power, yet if they approach their work without malice or an agenda, they can garner the continual respect of the arts community.

Arts writers and critics should be passionate about the art form they cover and be capable of backing up their opinions with solid, well-articulated facts. As journalists, they write under constant deadline pressure in a highly competitive arena—where scores of critic "wannabes" try to break into the field mainly as a means of getting free tickets to performances.

There are several freelance writing opportunities in this profession, as well as staff positions on newspapers and magazines. Today, it's a given that you have a computer and access to the Internet. Online arts publications continue to gain momentum.

Sensitive, congenial interviewing skills will take you a long way. When you're interviewing major celebrities and all types of artists, you must be prepared to encounter a surprising variety of responses. Be a good listener and observer and train yourself to think of responses and additional questions on the spot. You also constantly need to come up with fresh story ideas and pursue unique angles that will hold the public's interest.

Getting Started

The Internet and your area bookstore or library are enlightening places to start preparing for a career in arts writing and criticism. Scan the vast array of arts publications (and arts sections of daily, weekly, monthly, and quarterly newspapers and magazines) to get a feel for editorial style and content. Then subscribe to those publications that most interest you. Continue to study them and learn key industry terminology. Keep a file of some of the best-written articles and reviews.

Balance your high school curriculum with journalism, English literature, creative writing, and arts-related classes. Volunteer to write reviews of shows and concerts for your school newspaper. Or work part-time for a neighborhood newspaper that offers occasional opportunities to cover local productions.

Remember that critics at major publications do not vacate their positions readily. Some stay in the business for a lifetime. Well-paced timing, persistence, and a strong written voice are needed to prove your mettle in this niche writing market. Be patient and try to get as much writing experience as possible. Most importantly, get your byline out to the arts community. Editors are bound to notice your work, and more writing opportunities will follow.

Educational Requirements

Although the performing arts are your focus, the critical writing profession requires a liberal arts college degree in communication, journalism, or English. By also bringing to your resume a minor in any of the performing arts categories and experience in an arts-related occupation, you increase your chances of breaking into some of the big, well-respected publications.

As a writer-critic or arts editor, you must be able to express ideas clearly and logically—and with a flair for turning a creative phrase. Mastery of electronic publishing, graphics, and the Internet is essential.

A very popular and effective option for college journalism students is an internship experience at magazines, newspapers, and broadcast stations. These programs run in conjunction with college courses and offer credit toward a degree, combined with very practical experience that can lead to a full-time job. Some internships also pay. You will work alongside experienced professionals who can guide you in writing articles, doing research, and conducting interviews.

Getting Hired as an Arts Writer or Critic

Internships with magazines and newspapers are one of the most promising job-search tactics for arts writers and critics. Internships teach you the business and give you an opportunity to prove yourself capable of filling future job openings. Building a portfolio of poignant writing samples gives you a chance to perfect your craft and shows prospective editors your deep insights and sharp writing technique. Even if you are not assigned to review a performance, go anyway and write about it. Include these self-assigned critiques in your portfolio.

In order to get a firm grasp of the publishing industry, you need to work in that kind of environment—even if it's not arts-oriented. Entry-level positions as copywriters or assistant editors at weekly newspapers and trade and consumer magazines are smart starting points. Meanwhile, if the arts are your penchant, network at arts events to meet key decision makers. You may even learn of, say, a dance troupe in need of a newsletter editor.

When searching for an editorial job, research publications on the Internet or in person at bookstores and libraries. Make a list of the ones that most appeal to your interests and writing style. Find out current information on editors and when they are on deadline. Call to introduce yourself, or send a resume with writing samples, then follow up with another telephone call or an e-mail.

If you are determined enough and you happen to be a fabulous writer, editors will most likely appreciate your moxie. On the other hand, if no one is hiring full-time staff writers, go out and get your own stories, which you can try selling as a freelancer to these same publications.

As a freelance writer, you should be disciplined, self-motivated, and able to initiate projects on your own. While you have greater freedom and flexibility, you must constantly prove yourself through your outstanding reporting and writing ability. You don't earn a steady income, and you must balance your workload with expanding your presence in the arts writing arena. In other words, a continuing responsibility involves promoting yourself to editors and other prime decision makers in publishing.

Salary and Success Outlook for Arts Writers and Critics

Median annual earnings for salaried writers were $42,270 in 2000. The middle 50 percent earned between $29,090 and $57,330. The lowest 10 percent earned less than $20,290, and the highest 10 percent earned more than $81,370. Median annual earnings were $26,470 in the newspaper industry.

Freelance writers and critics are paid per story. With steady work, they can earn roughly a $30,000 to $40,000 annual salary, depending on the "stringer" (or nonstaff writer) budgets of certain publications.

Through 2010, the outlook for most writing and editing jobs is expected to remain competitive. Employment of salaried writers and editors is predicted to increase with growing demand for their publications. The high cost of paper and advancements in technology have paved the way for a new industry genre: online publications. These computer-based magazines can be found on the Internet and are replete with in-depth articles accompanied by full-color photographs and illustrations. However, online publications still struggle to attract advertisers, so writers should not expect to earn high fees. The bulk of their writing still feeds into print publications, which can offer more competitive salaries.

....

For More Information

American Society of Magazine Editors
919 Third Avenue, Twenty-Second Floor
New York, NY 10022
www.asme.magazine.org

International Association of Business Communicators
One Hallidic Plaza, Suite 600
San Francisco, CA 94102
www.iabc.com

The Newspaper Guild—Communication Workers of America
Research and Information Department
501 Third Street NW, Suite 250
Washington, DC 20001
www.newsguild.org

PR Reporter
Ragan Communications, Inc.
316 North Michigan Avenue, Suite 300
Chicago, IL 60601
www.ragan.com

Public Relations Society of America, Inc.
33 Irving Place
New York, NY 10003
www.prsa.org

Afterword

··

Careers in the performing arts are incredibly vast and multi-faceted. Although this book presents a detailed overview of the diverse opportunities available in this creative field, there are growing areas you may also wish to pursue.

In addition to the subdivisions discussed in this book, you can explore these related occupations: arts management, arts fundraising, director of government arts committees or organizations, arts advocacy (arts-related legal issues), and performing arts medicine (tending to the special medical needs of actors, dancers, singers, and musicians).

Explore the arts pages of the Internet, where technology enables artists to get up-to-the-minute information on new developments within the arts profession.

Finally, support your own local arts organizations. Attend theatrical performances and concerts. Volunteer for fund-raisers. In a world dominated by TVs, computers, and cell phones, the need for the live performing arts is more urgent. Individuals gathering together in a theatre promotes interaction and human contact—crucial elements no longer common in our increasingly high-tech society.

Additional Resources

Write to the organizations and institutions listed here to request information about careers in the performing arts or visit the websites for a wealth of information.

Arts Organizations

American Alliance for Health, Physical Education,
    Recreation and Dance
1900 Association Drive
Reston, VA 20191
www.aahperd.org

American Alliance for Theatre and Education
Department of Theater
Box 873411
Arizona State University
Tempe, AZ 85287
www.aate.com

American Dance Guild
P.O. Box 2006
Lenox Hill Station
New York, NY 10021
www.americandanceguild.org

Americans for the Arts
One East Fifty-Third Street
New York, NY 10022
www.artsusa.org

American Symphony Orchestra League
910 Seventeenth Street NW
Washington, DC 20006
www.symphony.org

Broadway Theatre Project
USF 30538
University of South Florida
4202 East Fowler Avenue
Tampa, FL 33620
www.broadwaytp.org

Center for Arts in the Basic Curriculum
725 Fifteenth Street NW, Suite 801
Washington, DC 20005

Chamber Music America
305 Seventh Avenue, Fifth Floor
New York, NY 10001
www.chamber-music.org

National Arts Education Association
1916 Association Drive
Reston, VA 20191
www.naea-reston.org

Dance/USA
1156 Fifteenth Street NW, Suite 820
Washington, DC 20005
www.danceusa.org

Educational Theatre Association
2343 Auburn Avenue
Cincinnati, OH 45219
www.edta.org

Folger Shakespeare Library
201 East Capitol Street SE
Washington, DC 20003
www.folger.edu

Foundation for Interior Design Education Research
146 Monroe Center NW, Suite 1318
Grand Rapids, MI 49503
www.fider.org

John F. Kennedy Center for the Performing Arts
2700 F Street NW
Washington, DC 20566
www.kennedy-center.org

National Association for Music Education
1806 Robert Fulton Drive
Reston, VA 20191
www.menc.org

National Endowment for the Arts
1100 Pennsylvania Avenue NW
Washington, DC 20506
www.nea.gov

National Foundation for Advancement in the Arts
800 Brickell Avenue, Suite 500
Miami, FL 33131
www.nfaa.org

International Network of Performing and Visual Arts Schools
173 Ridge View Drive
Berkeley Springs, WV 25411
www.artsschoolsnetwork.org

Opera America
1156 Fifteenth Street NW, Suite 810
Washington, DC 20005
www.operaam.org

Teachers and Writers Collaborative
5 Union Square West
New York, NY 10003
www.twc.org

Very Special Arts
1300 Connecticut Avenue NW, Suite 700
Washington, DC 20036
www.vsarts.org

Young Audiences
115 East Ninety-Second Street
New York, NY 10128
www.youngaudiences.org

....

Colleges and Universities

Augsburg College
2211 Riverside Avenue
Minneapolis, MN 55454
www.augsburg.edu

Augustana College
639 Thirty-Eighth Street
Rock Island, IL 61201
www.augustana.edu

Ball State University
Muncie, IN 47306
www.bsu.edu

Boston University
One Sherborn Street
Boston, MA 02215
www.bu.edu

Brandeis University
415 South Street
Waltham, MA 02454
www.brandeis.edu

California Institute of the Arts
24700 McBean Parkway
Valencia, CA 91355
www.calarts.edu

Columbia College Chicago
600 South Michigan Avenue
Chicago, IL 60605
www.colum.edu

Cornell University
Day Hal Lobby
Ithaca, NY 14853
www.cornell.edu

Dartmouth College
Hanover, NH 03755
www.dartmouth.edu

Dell'Arte School of Physical Theatre
P.O. Box 816
Blue Lake, CA 95525
www.dellarte.com

Drake University
2507 University Avenue
Des Moines, IA 50311
www.drake.edu

Emerson College
120 Boylston Street
Boston, MA 02116
www.emerson.edu

Hope College
Holland, MI 49423
www.hope.edu

Illinois State University
Campus Box 2200
Normal, IL 61790
www.ilstu.edu

Illinois Wesleyan University
1312 Park Street
Bloomington, IL 61701
www.iwu.edu

Indiana University
107 South Indiana Avenue
Bloomington, IN 47405
www.indiana.edu

Ithaca College
Ithaca, NY 14850
www.ithaca.edu

Lewis University
One University Parkway
Romeoville, IL 60446
www.lewisu.edu

Loyola University Chicago
6525 North Sheridan Road
Chicago, IL 60626
www.luc.edu

Millikin University
1184 West Main Street
Decatur, IL 62522
www.millikin.edu

Minnesota State University, Mankato
Mankato, MN 56001
www.mankato.msus.edu

New York University
Tisch School of the Arts
721 Broadway
New York, NY 10003
www.nyu.edu/tisch

Northeastern Illinois University
5500 North Saint Louis Avenue
Chicago, IL 60625
www.neiu.edu

Northern Illinois University
DeKalb, IL 60115
www.niu.edu

Northwestern University
633 Clark Street
Evanston, IL 60208
www.northwestern.edu

Ohio University
Athens, OH 45701
www.ohio.edu

Purchase College (SUNY)
735 Anderson Hill Road
Purchase, NY 10577
www.purchase.edu

Purdue University
West Lafayette, IN 47907
www.purdue.edu

Roosevelt University
430 South Michigan Avenue
Chicago, IL 60605
www.roosevelt.edu

Southern Illinois University, Carbondale
Carbondale, IL 62901
www.siu.edu

The Theatre School, DePaul University
One East Jackson
Chicago, IL 60614
www.depaul.edu

University at Buffalo (SUNY)
Undergraduate Admissions
17 Capen Hall
Buffalo, NY 14260
www.buffalo.edu

University of Alabama
Tuscaloosa, AL 35487
www.ua.edu

University of Arizona
Tucson, AZ 85721
www.arizona.edu

University of California, Berkeley
Berkeley, CA 94720
www.berkeley.edu

University of California, Los Angeles
405 Hilgard Avenue
Los Angeles, CA 90095
www.ucla.edu

University of California, San Diego
5998 Alcalá Park
San Diego, CA 92110
www.sandiego.edu

University of California, Santa Barbara
Santa Barbara, CA 93106
www.ucsb.edu

University of Evansville
1800 Lincoln Avenue
Evansville, IN 47722
www.evansville.edu

University of Florida
Gainesville, FL 32611
www.ufl.edu

University of Houston
4800 Calhoun Road
Houston, TX 77204
www.uh.edu

University of Illinois at Urbana
901 West Illinois Street
Urbana, IL 61801
www.uiuc.edu

University of Iowa
Iowa City, IA 52242
www.uiowa.edu

University of Missouri, Kansas City
4949 Cherry Street
Kansas City, MO 64110
www.umkc.edu

University of North Carolina
Chapel Hill, NC 27599
www.unc.edu

University of Texas at Austin
Austin, TX 78712
www.utexas.edu

University of Toledo
Toledo, OH 43606
www.utoledo.edu

University of Washington
Seattle, WA 98195
www.washington.edu

Valparaiso University
Valparaiso, IN 46383
www.valpo.edu

Wayne State University
Detroit, MI 48202
www.wayne.edu

Western Illinois University
One University Circle
Macomb, IL 61455
www.wiu.edu

Yale University School of Drama
P.O. Box 208325
New Haven, CT 06520
www.yale.edu/drama

About the Author

Lucia Mauro has been writing about the performing arts throughout Chicagoland since 1988. She is a dance/theatre critic and arts writer whose work appears in the *Chicago Tribune, Chicago Magazine, North Shore Magazine, PerformInk, Stage Directions, Dance Magazine, Dance Teacher,* and *Dance Spirit*; on her website www.chicagotheater.com; and more.

A lover of all art forms, Mauro studied classical ballet for most of her life and also plays the piano. She holds a bachelor's degree summa cum laude in English and communications from Loyola University Chicago.

Mauro is a guest arts commentator on Chicago's WGN and WBEZ radio, and she appears on *The Career Clinic,* a syndicated radio show based in Minneapolis. She has been a guest on WTTW-TV's *Artbeat,* serves on many arts panels, and is invited by numerous arts groups as a keynote speaker. Mauro received the James Friend Memorial Award for Outstanding Theatre Criticism and was voted one of one hundred Women Making a Difference in Chicago by *Today's Chicago Woman* magazine.

Careers for the Stagestruck & Other Dramatic Types marks her third book for McGraw-Hill. She penned VGM's *Career Portraits: Fashion* and *Careers for Fashion Plates & Other Trendsetters.* The author lives with her husband, Joe Orlandino, in the heart of Chicago's off-Loop theatre district, where most of their evenings are spent front-row, center—just a breath away from the footlights.

791
MAU

Mauro, Lucia.

Careers for the
stagestruck & other
dramatic types.

32786000372280

$12.95

Mauro, Lucia.

Careers for the
stagestruck &
other dramatic
types.

32786000372280

$12.95

DATE	BORROWER'S NAME	

BAKER & TAYLOR